IMAGES 2

English for Beginners

Guenther Zuern

▲▼ Addison-Wesley Publishing Company

Reading, Massachusetts • Menlo Park, California
Don Mills, Ontario • Wokingham, England • Amsterdam • Bonn • Sydney
Singapore • Tokyo • Madrid • Bogota • Santiago • San Juan

A publication of the World Language Division

Dedicated to Colette Whiten and Paul Kipps

Special thanks to Heather Marshall, Robin Bennett and the many individuals who permitted themselves or their places of business to be photographed.

Acknowledgments

Editorial: *Kathleen Sands Boehmer and Elly Schottman*
Manufacturing/Production: *James W. Gibbons*
Photographs: *Guenther Zuern,* except:

  page 35, photo A and page 37, photo 3—Heather Marshall
  page 65, photo A—courtesy of New York Convention and
    Visitors Bureau
  page 65, photo C—courtesy of Canada Post Corporation
  page 65, photo D—courtesy of Canadian Imperial Bank of
    Commerce

Photo layout design: *Guenther Zuern*

Illustrations: *Susan Avishai and Laura Maine*

Cover design: *Marshall Henrichs*

IJ-AL-89
ISBN: 0-201-09807-5

TO THE TEACHER

INTRODUCING *IMAGES*

IMAGES 1 & 2: English for Beginners is a visually exciting series for adult and young adult learners of English. Each lesson in *IMAGES* presents a practical, real-life situation through a full-page story sequence of photographs. The photos immediately capture the students' interest and clarify the meaning and context of the language. Each photo presentation is followed by a practice page containing a variety of exercises reinforcing the functions and structures introduced in the lesson and offering opportunities for communicative activities. A Review and Discover section after every six lessons provides additional review as well as vocabulary enrichment. An accompanying tape program offers an integrated listening skills strand.

WHO IS IT FOR?

IMAGES is designed to be equally effective in a variety of learning situations: whole class instruction, individualized instruction in a multi-level classroom, or independent study in a language lab or at home. Vocabulary and structures are presented in a clear, carefully controlled manner. Each lesson introduces only a select number of new lexical and structural items, carefully integrated with previously introduced material.

IMAGES 1 has been particularly developed for the student who has no previous knowledge of English. *IMAGES 2* is a continuation of *IMAGES 1,* and takes the student through the beginner level to the advanced beginner/intermediate stage. The presentation of language through realistic dialogues and the emphasis on meaningful oral practice makes *IMAGES 2* an ideal introductory text for the false beginner with a more than basic passive knowledge of English.

HOW DOES IT WORK?

Two questions served as guidelines and criteria for determining the content of *IMAGES*: 1) What do non-English speakers most immediately need to understand and express in order to cope in an English-speaking environment? 2) What is the most direct and natural form in which these language skills can be taught and learned? Functions and notions were selected according to the first criterion. A photographic format, conveying real-life situations through conversations and narratives, was chosen in answer to the second question. Lessons were then developed, linked to a thoughtful structural grading of the material. The resulting program, *IMAGES,* thus offers beginning students unique access to English both from a functional perspective (what they need to understand and express) and from a grammatical perspective (what they need to generate their own language).

Stumbling blocks to comprehension are minimized in *IMAGES* by the gradual introduction of new vocabulary, and the clear conveyance of meaning through the photographs. This facilitates the students' recognition of the structural patterns and rules that are at work. Highlighted excerpts illustrating these rules aid this discovery process. Communicative use of the language is fostered by practice exercises which provide ample opportunity for pair work and role play. The emphasis is on students using grammar to create language that suits their needs.

COMPONENTS OF THE *IMAGES 2* PROGRAM

THE STUDENT BOOK—36 clearly designed and carefully sequenced lessons teach and reinforce a balance of functions and structures through photographic presentations of real-life situations. An answer key, which can be removed at the teacher's discretion, is provided at the back of the student book.

THE TEACHER'S EDITION—A 16-page guide for the classroom teacher, offering suggestions for expanding and reinforcing each lesson, precedes a full-size reprint of the student book. Texts for the unscripted listening comprehension activities found on the tapes are provided for teachers who wish to incorporate the developmental listening skill strand into their program but do not have access to the tapes.

THE TAPE PROGRAM—Two cassettes accompany *IMAGES 2.* The dialogue or narrative from each photo presentation page is recorded in several ways for listening, practice, and role play. There are four simple instructions that students need to learn in order to respond to the listening activities: "Listen." "Listen and repeat." "Let's have a conversation. I begin." "Let's have a conversation. You begin." In addition, the tapes present an important unscripted listening skills strand. A small illustration on each Review page and at the bottom of every third lesson in the student text reminds the student (and teacher) that a listening comprehension activity is available on the tape. The format follows a clear pattern which students can learn easily. Thus, there are no difficulties for students using the program independently.

HOW TO USE THIS BOOK

Individualized Instruction and Independent Study

IMAGES 2 is ideally suited for use by students in a multi-level classroom, or for independent practice and study in the language lab or at home. The method is simple, and easily conveyed to the student by means of the instructions on the tape, or a short demonstration by the teacher.

Each lesson opens with a photo presentation introducing the new functions, vocabulary and structures. The student begins by reading the photo presentation and listening to the conversation or narration on the tape cassette. He or she repeats the dialogue lines after the actors, practicing pronunciation and inflection. When comfortable, the student turns to the second page of the lesson. The following exercise formats are used:

Dictionary. This exercise involves writing down the translation of the key new words introduced in the lesson. Since the meaning of these new words is often conveyed by the photos, the use of a bilingual dictionary is optional, depending on the student's need for confirmation and reinforcement.

Practice A. This cloze exercise reproduces the lesson text but leaves strategic blanks to be filled in by the student. To correct his or her work, the student simply turns back to the original photo presentation page.

Partners Exercise.
A symbol representing the *Partners* exercise appears after *Practice A* in each lesson. In the individualized or independent study approach, the tape serves as the student's partner. In most lessons, the tape instructs the student to assume the role of one of the characters in the photo presentation and role play the dialogue, responding to the taped lines of the other character(s). Other lessons require students to respond to questions about the photo presentation.

Practice B, C, D and E. Each lesson offers several additional writing exercises to reinforce new and recycled material. Answers to the exercises can be checked against the Answer Key provided at the end of the student book.

Listening Activities. A cassette symbol, found at the end of Lessons 3, 9, 15, 21, 27 and 33, and on all Review pages, alerts the student to the fact that a *Listening Activity* is provided on the tape. Responses to the *Listening Activities* on the Review pages are to be written in the spaces provided in the student book. Responses to the *Listening Activities* at the end of the other lessons are to be written on a separate piece of paper. The answers to all the *Listening Activities* are included in the Answer Key.

Whole Class or Teacher-Directed Instruction

The following is a suggested method for presenting each lesson in *IMAGES 2* in a whole class or teacher-directed situation. Feel free to adapt and vary the presentation according to the needs of your class and your own teaching style. The Teacher's Edition provides suggestions for large and small-group activities designed to expand and reinforce each lesson and to enhance the communicative potential of classroom instruction.

1. Play the tape or read the photo presentation aloud two or three times while students read along in their books. This provides the students with an initial pronunciation model. The photographs help clarify the meaning and the context of the text.

2. Allow time for students to read the photo presentation on their own. Students may ask each other questions, translate, refer to dictionaries, or do whatever they feel is necessary to comprehend the material. Test the students' comprehension by asking questions about the photo presentation. Encourage discussion of such things as the content of the photos, the situation depicted, the appropriateness of certain responses, and other related topics.

3. Play the tape or read the photo presentation aloud again. Students then repeat each dialogue line, either chorally and/or individually. Then, have students assume roles, and read the lines of their respective characters in the dialogue.

4. The students turn to the practice page. The *Dictionary* exercise provides space for students to jot down notes on the meaning and/or pronunciation of key new words and phrases in the text. *Practice A,* a cloze exercise of the lesson text, may be completed in the manner you stipulate, or in the way each student finds personally most effective. The student can choose to correct after each blank or at the end of the exercise. *Practice A* may also be completed as a dictation exercise in which students listen to the original text read by the teacher (or tape) and fill in the blanks.

5. *Partners Exercise.*
This symbol, appearing below *Practice A* in each lesson, represents the *Partners* exercise. Students practice the dialogue with a partner, taking turns playing each role. Encourage students to read with appropriate expression and gestures. In lessons which are presented as a narrative, the *Partners* exercise can require students to retell the narrative in their own words or ask their partners questions about the narrative.

6. *Practice B, C. D and E.* These exercises are most effectively completed as pair work. Most exercises are designed to be done first orally and then in writing as reinforcement of the oral production. However, you may wish to have the students write all, or only part of an exercise before initiating oral practice. Some exercises are intended for writing practice only in order to reinforce the lexical or structural priorities of the lesson. Encourage partners to discuss and compare their answers and to assist each other with problems.

7. *Listening Activities.* Indicated by a cassette symbol in every Review Lesson and at the end of Lessons 3, 9, 15, 21, 27, and 33, these taped activities provide a variety of skill-building exercises focusing on auditory discrimination and aural comprehension. The scripts of the *Listening Activities* are provided in the Teacher's Edition for teachers who do not own the tapes but wish to construct their own version of the listening skill strand.

CONTENTS

LESSON		FUNCTIONS AND STRUCTURES
21	When will he be home?	Request/Give information over the telephone; leave a message; make an appointment; make a collect call; future: *will, won't*; future adverbials.
22	I have to	Call in sick to work and give reasons; ask permission; express hope/ sympathy; modals: *can't, have to*.
23	When can you do it?	Ask about/State obligations and possibilities; make/decline a suggestion; *has to*
24	You should	Talk to a doctor about your health, give advice; modals: *should, shouldn't*; present perfect: *How long have you been . . . ?*
	Review and Discover	Review lessons 19–24; listening comprehension; talk about health problems and remedies.
25	What's the weather like?	Ask/Talk about the weather; *to be*: present, past and future forms.
26	What time will it leave?	Request/Give information about airline reservations and hotel accommodations; order a taxi; integration of modals, present tense and future.
27	Yesterday I went to . . .	Ask/Talk about past activities; past tense forms of irregular verbs: *went, had, bought, met, paid, were*.
28	A wonderful trip.	Ask/Talk about a past vacation; past tense forms of regular and irregular verbs.
29	Where were you?	Request/Give information in a bank/post office; talk about past activities; *to be*: past tense forms; indirect object: sentence patterns with *to* and *for*.
30	What are you going to do?	Ask/Talk about plans; future: *going to*.
	Review and Discover	Review lessons 25–30; listening comprehension; dialogues about past activities.
31	How much will it cost?	Request/Give information at a gas station; offer to do something; contrast: *going to* (intent) vs. *will* (offer).
32	How does it look?	Request/Give information and advice about buying clothes; contrast: *I'm going to . . .* (certain) vs. *Maybe I'll . . .* (uncertain); two-part verbs: *Try on the jacket. Try it on.*
33	What size do you wear?	Request information from a salesperson; make comparisons; comparative form of adjectives: *bigger, smaller*.
34	Can you lend me . . . ?	Compare items in a store; ask about prices; return a defective purchase; comparative forms: *more/less expensive, as good as*.
35	At the supermarket.	Talk about food; ask for/give directions in a supermarket; count vs. non-count nouns; *How much . . . ?* vs. *How many . . . ?*
36	Sorry, we don't have any	Order food in a restaurant; instruct someone on how to use a vending machine; *some* vs. *any*; indefinite pronouns: *something, anything, nothing, everything*.
	Review and Discover	Review lessons 31–36; listening comprehension; ask/talk about mechanical problems with a car; expressions of quantity.

How are you doing?

Hello, Tom.

Hi, Linda. How are you doing?

Fine, thanks.

Tom, I'd like you to meet my friend, Kim.

Nice to meet you.

Nice to meet you, too.

Kim is new in Boston. She's from Tokyo.

How do you like it here?

It's very nice, but I miss Tokyo. All my family is there. How about you? Are you from Boston?

No, I'm from New York, but most of my friends are here in Boston.

1

I would like ||||➡ I'd like   here ☞ ■   there ☞ ····■

Dictionary

all _____   most _____
miss _____   there _____

Practice A

★ Hello, Tom.

○ Hi, Linda. How are you _doing_ ?

★ Fine, thanks.

  Tom, I'd _____ you to meet my friend, Kim.

○ Nice to _____ you.

■ Nice to _____ you, _____ .

★ Kim is _____ in Boston. She's _____ Tokyo.

○ How do you like it _____ ?

■ It's very nice, but I _____ Tokyo. All my family is _____ . How about you?

  _____ you from Boston?

○ No, I'm from New York, but _____ of my friends _____ here in Boston.

Practice B

1. wife / Los Angeles / San Francisco
   ★ _Is your wife from Los Angeles_ ?
   ○ _No, she's from San Francisco_ .

2. brother / Tokyo / Osaka
   _____ ?
   _____ .

3. your girl friend / Mexico City / Acapulco
   _____ ?
   _____ .

4. you / New York / _____
   _____ ?
   _____ .

5. most of your friends / Boston / _____
   _____ ?
   _____ .

6. the teacher / Miami / _____
   _____ ?
   _____ .

7. your parents / Chicago / _____
   _____ ?
   _____ .

Practice C

Write these conversations on a piece of paper.

1. brother / Boston / New York
   ★ _Is your brother in Boston?_
   ○ _No, he isn't._
   ★ _Oh, where is he?_
   ○ _He's in New York._

2. sister / Hong Kong / Singapore
3. parents / Brazil / Argentina
4. boyfriend / England / France
5. _____ / _____ / _____

Practice D

1. Where are you from?
   _____

2. Where is your family?
   _____

3. Where are most of your friends?
   _____

4. How do you like your city?
   _____

What do you do?

What floor do you live on?

1st	2nd	3rd	4th	5th	6th	7th	8th	9th	10th
first	second	third	fourth	fifth	sixth	seventh	eighth	ninth	tenth

Dictionary

alone _____   engineer _____   live _____   part-time _____

do (verb) _____   floor _____   office _____   work _____

Practice A

★ What do you _do_ , Tom?

○ I'm an engineer. And you?

★ I _____ economics at the university, and I _____ part-time.

○ Where _____ _____ work?

★ _____ an office _____ Bay Street.

· · · · · · · · · · · · · ·

★ Well, this is my_____ .

○ Do you _____ in an apartment?

★ Yes, I have a small apartment on the tenth _____ .

○ Do you live _____ ?

★ No, I live _____ my friend.

○ See you _____ , Kim.

★ Bye. _____ a nice day.

Practice B

Write these conversations on a piece of paper.

1. doctor / hospital / Tenth St.
   ★ *What do you do?*
   ○ *I'm a doctor.*
   ★ *Where do you work?*
   ○ *In a hospital on Tenth St.*
2. mechanic / garage / Bedford Rd.
3. waitress / restaurant / Lakeshore Ave.
4. cashier / hardware store / Front St.
5. _____ / _____ / _____

Practice C

Write these conversations on a piece of paper.

1. small / 9th / friend
   ★ *Do you live in an apartment?*
   ○ *Yes, I have a small apartment on the ninth floor.*
   ★ *Do you live alone?*
   ○ *No, I live with my friend.*
2. big / 5th / family
3. small / 3rd / husband and daughter
4. nice / 2nd / sister
5. _____ / _____ / _____

Practice D

1. What do you do?

_____

2. Where do you work?

_____

3. Where do you study English?

_____

4. Do you live in an apartment or a house?

_____

5. What floor do you live on?

_____

6. Who do you live with?

_____

Where do you live?

Dictionary

Do you mind if . . . _____
come _____   seat _____
often _____   sit _____

Practice A

★ Is this _seat_ _____ taken?

○ No.

★ Do you _____ if I sit here?

○ _____ you like.

★ _____ I buy you a cup of coffee?

○ No, thanks. I _____ one.

★ _____ _____ come here often?

○ No, I _____ .

★ _____ _____ live in Boston?

○ No.

★ Oh, _____ do you live?

○ New York.

★ New York! _____ _____ like New York?

○ Yes, I _____ .

But I _____ like you!

Practice B

Do you . . . ?   Are you . . . ?

1. _Do you_ _____ live in Miami?   No, _I don't_ .
2. _____ married?   Yes, _____ .
3. _____ have a car?   Yes, _____ .
4. _____ work in an office?   No, _____ .
5. _____ an engineer?   No, _____ .
6. _____ hungry?   Yes, _____ .
7. _____ live alone?   Yes, _____ .

Practice C

What?   Where?   Who?   How?

1. _Where do you work_ ?   I work in a restaurant.
2. _____ ?   I live on the first floor.
3. _____ ?   I live with my brother.
4. _____ ?   I'm from Japan.
5. _____ ?   I live in Chicago.
6. _____ ?   I study English.
7. _____ ?   Fine, thanks.

Practice D

1. I live <u>in</u> Canada. (country)
2. I live <u>in</u> Ottawa. (city)
3. I live <u>on</u> Elm Street. (street)
4. I live <u>at</u> 265 Elm Street. (address)

Where do you live?

_____ . (country)

_____ . (city)

_____ . (street)

_____ . (address)

Practice E

at, in, on

1. I live _in_ _____ an apartment.
2. I live _____ New York.
3. I study _____ the university.
4. I live _____ Tenth Street.
5. What floor do you live _____ ?
6. They work _____ 300 Shaw Street.
7. They're _____ the United States.

We like different things.

I like vanilla ice cream. My husband likes chocolate.

I drink coffee, but my wife prefers tea.

In my spare time I like to read books. He likes to read magazines.

I have a bicycle. She has a car.

We like different things, but we are happy together.

A. ★ What kind of ice cream do you like?
   ○ I like chocolate.
   ★ What kind of ice cream does your wife like?
   ○ She likes vanilla.

B. ★ What do you like to do in your spare time?
   ■ I like to read.
   ★ What does your husband like to do in his spare time?
   ■ He likes to ride his bicycle.

I		He	I have.......	He/She has.........
You	verb...	She verb + s...	I go..........	He/She goes ....
We		It	I study......	He/She studies....
They				

Dictionary

different _____   prefer _____   ride _____   thing _____
magazine _____   read _____   spare time _____   together _____

Practice A

★ I _____ vanilla ice cream. My husband _____ chocolate.

○ I _____ coffee, but my wife _____ tea.

★ In my _____ time I _____ to read books. He _____ to read magazines.

○ I _____ a bicycle. She _____ a car.

★ We like _____ things, but we _____ happy together.

A. ★ What kind of ice cream _____ you _____ ?

  ○ I _____ chocolate.

  ★ What kind of ice cream _____ your wife _____ ?

  ○ She _____ vanilla.

B. ★ What _____ you like _____ do in your spare time?

  ■ I like _____ read.

  ★ What _____ your husband like _____ _____ in his spare time?

  ■ He _____ to ride his bicycle.

Practice B

Answer these questions about the photo story.

1. What kind of ice cream does his wife like?
_____

2. What kind of ice cream does her husband like?
_____

3. What does he like to drink?
_____

4. Does his wife prefer tea or coffee?
_____

5. What does she like to do in her spare time?
_____

6. Does her husband have a car or a bicycle?
_____

7. Are they happy?
_____

Practice C

1. Are you happy?
_____

2. What do you like to do in your spare time?
_____

3. What do you like to eat?
_____

Practice D

1. want   She _wants_ a new car.
2. need   They _____ more money.
3. go   He _____ to bed at ten o'clock.
4. like   They _____ different things.
5. have   She _____ three children.
6. drive   He _____ a taxi in New York.
7. drink   We _____ coffee in the morning.
8. buy   I _____ food at the supermarket.
9. work   My sister _____ in an office.

10. pay   I _____ two dollars for a gallon of gas.
11. live   Maria _____ with her husband.
12. speak   You _____ English very well.
13. come   My parents _____ here often.
14. study   Kim _____ economics.
15. get up   I _____ at six thirty.
16. eat   Tom _____ lunch in a restaurant.
17. know   We _____ his brother-in-law.

8

That machine doesn't work.

That machine doesn't work. Use this one.

Does it work?

I think so.

Do you usually come to this laundromat?

No, I don't. My wife usually washes clothes, but she doesn't have time now. She has a new job.

Does she like her job?

Yes, she does.

Do you like this job?

I'm not sure.

> ☞ He like_s_ this job.   She _has_ a new job.   I wash clothes. = I do the laundry.
> Doe_s_ he like this job?   Does she _have_ a new job?   I was_h_ .....   He/She wash_es_ .....

Dictionary

clothes _____   think _____
job _____   use _____
machine _____   usually _____
now _____   wash _____

I	he
Do you [verb] . . . ?	Does she [verb] . . . ?
we	it
they	
Yes, I do./No, I don't.	Yes, she does./No, she doesn't.

Practice A

★ That machine _____ work. _____ this one.

○ _____ it work?

★ I think so.

★ _____ you usually _____ to this laundromat?

○ No, I _____ . My wife usually washes clothes, but she _____ have time now. She _____ a new job.

★ _____ she _____ her job?

○ Yes, she _____ .

★ _____ you _____ this job?

○ I'm _____ sure.

Practice C

don't, doesn't, isn't, aren't

1. He _isn't_ rich. He _____ have any money.

2. They _____ speak Japanese. They _____ from Japan.

3. She _____ happy because she _____ have a job.

4. I'm not sure because I _____ understand the teacher.

5. The price _____ $3.98. It's $2.98.

6. Those shoes _____ very expensive.

7. This bus _____ go to Tenth Street.

8. I _____ like Maria because she _____ friendly.

9. _____ use that pen. It _____ work.

10. She _____ want another baby. One is enough.

Practice B

1. _Do you like to do the laundry_ ?
   Yes, I like to do the laundry.

2. _____ ?
   Yes, my wife has a new job.

3. _____ ?
   Yes, I usually come here.

4. _____ ?
   Yes, Kim studies economics.

5. _____ ?
   Yes, I miss my family and friends.

6. _____ ?
   Yes, my friends live in New York.

7. _____ ?
   Yes, my brother likes to read.

8. _____ ?
   Yes, that machine works.

9. _____ ?
   Yes, my daughter needs some medicine.

10. _____ ?
    Yes, my parents speak English.

Practice D

1. Who washes your clothes?

   _____

2. Do you wash your clothes at home or at a laundromat?

   _____

3. Do you wash your clothes by hand or do you use a washing machine?

   _____

4. Do you like to do the laundry?

   _____

10

How do I get to . . . ?

A

★ How do I get to Lakeside Park?

○ Take the University subway line west. Get off at Rosedale, then transfer to the number 42 bus south.

★ How do I get to the Royal Museum?

○ Take the number 13 bus north. Get off at Main Street, then walk three blocks east.

B

★ Excuse me. Is there a laundromat near here?

○ Yes, there's one just up the street.

★ How far is it?

○ About three and a half blocks. It's across from the supermarket.

C

★ What time is the next bus to Vancouver?

○ At 10:30. It leaves in half an hour.

★ What time does it arrive in Vancouver?

○ At 11:30.

★ Can I have two tickets, please?

There is ▷ There's

Dictionary

arrive _____   half _____
far _____   leave _____
get off _____   near _____
get to _____   transfer _____

Practice A

A. ★ How do I _____ to Lakeside Park?

   ○ _____ the University subway line west.
   Get _____ at Rosedale, then
   _____ to the number 42 bus south.

B. ★ Excuse me. Is _____ a laundromat
   _____ here?

   ○ Yes, _____ one just up the street.

   ★ How _____ is it?

   ○ About three and a half _____ . It's
   _____ from the supermarket.

C. ★ What time is the _____ bus to Vancouver?

   ○ _____ 10:30. It _____ in half
   an hour.

   ★ What time does it _____ in Vancouver?

   ○ _____ 11:30.

   ★ Can I _____ two tickets, please?

Practice B

Write these conversations on a piece of paper.

1.

★ How do I get to High Park?
○ Take the Victoria subway line west. Get off at Fifth Avenue. Then transfer to the number 77 bus south.

2.

3.

4.

5.

Practice C

Write these conversations on a piece of paper.

1. supermarket / 2½ blocks / next to the bus station
   ★ Excuse me. Is there a supermarket near here?
   ○ Yes. There's one just up the street.
   ★ How far is it?
   ○ About two and a half blocks. It's next to the bus station.

2. bank / ½ a block / across from the hotel

3. gas station / 2 blocks / on the corner of Main and West St.

4. drug store / 3 blocks / between the library and the church

5. laundromat / _____ / _____

Practice D

Write these conversations on a piece of paper.

1. flight / Montreal / 9:30 / an hour / 11:30
   ★ What time is the next flight to Montreal?
   ○ At nine thirty. It leaves in an hour.
   ★ What time does it arrive in Montreal?
   ○ At eleven thirty.

2. train / New York / 1:45 / ½ an hour / 4:00

3. bus / Los Angeles / 8:30 / 20 minutes / midnight

4. train / Dallas / 9:15 / 10 minutes / noon

5. bus / _____ / _____ / _____ / _____

REVIEW/Lessons 1-6

WHICH ONE IS IT?

1. a. Does he live in New York?
   b. Does she live in New York?

2. a. She has a new teacher.
   b. She is a new teacher.

3. a. Where do you live?
   b. When do you leave?

4. a. What time does it arrive?
   b. What time does he arrive?

5. a. Is this the tenth floor?
   b. Is it on the tenth floor?

6. a. Do you mind if I sit here?
   b. Do you mind if I sit there?

7. a. Are these seats taken?
   b. Is this seat taken?

8. a. It leaves in half an hour.
   b. It leaves in an hour.

9. a. Does she come here often?
   b. Doesn't she come here often?

YES OR NO?

1. Does Susan usually go to the restaurant?	YES	NO
2. Does Susan usually eat at home?	YES	NO
3. Does Susan like coffee?	YES	NO
4. Does Bob work at the restaurant all day?	YES	NO
5. Does Bob like his job?	YES	NO
6. Does Susan have a job?	YES	NO
7. Does she work in a hardware store?	YES	NO
8. Does she work downtown?	YES	NO

MATCH THE SENTENCES.

1. What time is the next bus to Denver? __d__

2. Are you from Boston? _____

3. Do you live alone? _____

4. Does your wife like her job? _____

5. Is your wife a teacher? _____

6. Where do you work? _____

7. What do you do? _____

8. What do you study? _____

a. No, I'm from Toronto.

b. No, she doesn't.

c. Yes, she is.

d. At 8:30.

e. English

f. I'm a mechanic.

g. Yes, I do.

h. In a garage on Beach St.

DISCOVER/Lessons 1–6

Discover A

Donna is a dentist. She works in a clinic in downtown Boston. She likes her job a lot. In her spare time she likes to play tennis.

Dan is a construction worker. He works outside all day. He doesn't like the job because the work is very hard. In the evening he likes to watch TV. His favorite program is Police Story.

Frank is a salesman at the Looking Good clothing store. He likes his job. In the evenings he likes to play cards with his friends.

Monica is a nurse at the Toronto General Hospital. She is unhappy with her job because she works at night. On the weekends she likes to cook Chinese food for her family.

Teresa is a secretary for a large electronics company. She wants a new job because she doesn't like her supervisor. After work she likes to listen to music. She likes rock music.

Peter is a singer in a nightclub in Las Vegas. When he has spare time, he likes to play the guitar or to take photographs.

1. What does Donna do?
_____

2. Where does she work?
_____

3. What does she like to do in her spare time?
_____

4. What does Frank sell?
_____

5 Does Teresa work outside?
_____

6. Does Teresa work during the day or at night?
_____

7. Why does she want a new job?
_____

8. What does Dan like to do in the evening?
_____

9. When does Monica sleep? Why?
_____

10. What does Peter do?
_____

11. Does he work during the day or at night?
_____

12. Does Peter have a camera?
_____

Discover B

1. What do you like to do in your spare time?
_____

2. What does your friend like to do in his / her spare time?
_____

3. What is your favorite TV program?
_____

4. What kind of music do you like?
_____

5. Do you play the guitar or some other musical instrument?
_____

6. What kind of food do you like to eat or cook?
_____

Do you have a job?

1. Hi, George.
Hi, Pat.

2. Hey, what's this?
Do you have a job now?
Yes.

3. What do you do?
I'm a machine operator in a factory on King Street.

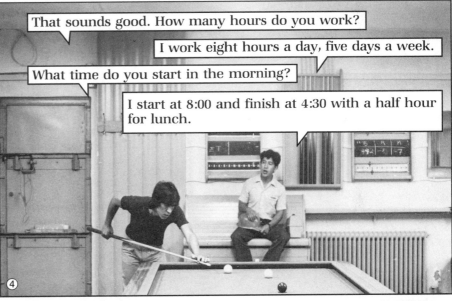

4. That sounds good. How many hours do you work?
I work eight hours a day, five days a week.
What time do you start in the morning?
I start at 8:00 and finish at 4:30 with a half hour for lunch.

5. So, how much do you make?

6. Ten dollars an hour.

7. That's great! Congratulations!

15

☞ I finish . . .   He/She finish**es**

Practice A

★ Hi, Pat.

○ Hi, George.

★ Hey, what's this? Do you have a _____ now?

○ Yes.

★ What _____ you _____ ?

○ I'm a machine operator in a _____ on King Street.

★ That sounds good. _____ _____ hours do you work?

○ I work eight hours _____ day, five days _____ week.

★ What time do you _____ in the morning?

○ I _____ at 8:00 and _____ at 4:30 with a _____ hour for lunch.

★ So, how _____ do you _____ ?

○ Ten dollars an hour.

★ That's great! _____ !

Dictionary

congratulations _____   finish _____
factory _____   hour _____
make _____   start _____
operator _____   thousand _____

Practice B

Answer these questions about the photo story.

1. What does George do?

_____

2. Where does he work?

_____

3. How many hours does he work a day?

_____

4. How many hours does he work a week?

_____

5. What time does he start work?

_____

6. What time does he finish work?

_____

7. How much does he make?

_____

Practice C

1. *What do you do* _____ ?
   I'm a secretary.

2. _____ ?
   I work in an office on Jefferson Avenue.

3. _____ ?
   I work nine hours a day.

4. _____ ?
   I start at eight thirty.

5. _____ ?
   I make three hundred dollars a week.

6. _____ ?
   Donna is a dentist.

7. _____ ?
   She works thirty-six hours a week.

8. _____ ?
   She finishes work at 4:30.

9. _____ ?
   She makes thirty-five thousand dollars a year.

10. _____ ?
    Yes, she likes her job.

11. _____ ?
    No, I'm not a teacher. I'm a student.

12. _____ ?
    I start school at 9:30.

Practice D

1. Are you a student or do you have a job?

_____

2. What time do you start school / work?

_____

3. What time do you finish school / work?

_____

4. How many hours do you study / work a week?

_____

Monday morning.

One regular coffee to go, please.

Monday morning! Time to get up! Every Monday it's the same thing.
I get up early because it takes me about an hour to get to work.
I take the bus and then the subway. The subway is usually crowded.

I feel tired. I need a cup of coffee.

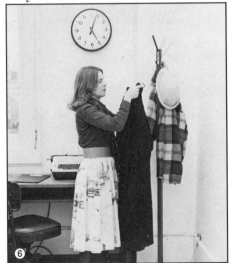

Oh, no! I'm already late.
Why is this elevator so slow?

Sorry I'm late, Mr. Davis.

Don't be late again!

He's angry because this is the third time this month.

I finish work at five o'clock. I'm always happy when it's time to go home. I sometimes go for a walk
in the park after work. I go to the park to relax because Mondays are never good days for me.

17

> ☞ regular coffee = coffee with cream and sugar
> black coffee = no cream
> How long does it take you to get to work? = How much time does it take you to get to work?

★ How do you get to work?	never	⎰	0%
○ I take the subway.	sometimes	⎰	50%
or	usually	⎰	75%
○ I get to work by subway.	always	⎰	100%

Practice A

Monday morning! Time _____ get up!

_____ Monday it's the same thing. I get up

_____ because it _____ me about an

hour to _____ to work. I _____ the

bus and then the subway. The subway is

_____ crowded.

I _____ tired. I need a cup of coffee.

"One regular coffee _____ _____ please."

Oh, no! I'm already _____ . Why is this

elevator so _____ ?

"_____ , I'm late, Mr. Davis."

"Don't _____ late again!"

He's angry because this is the third _____
this month.

I _____ work at five o'clock. I'm _____

happy when it's time _____ _____ home.

I sometimes go for a _____ in the park after

_____ . I go to the park to _____

because Mondays are _____ good days for me.

Practice C

(i) eat, get up, go, have, start

1. It's time to *get up* .
2. It's time to _____ dinner.
3. It's time to _____ a cup of coffee.
4. It's time to _____ the English class.
5. It's time to _____ home.

(ii) buy, make, read, relax, study

1. I go for a walk in the park to *relax* .
2. I go to school to _____ English.
3. I go to the library to _____ books.
4. I work to _____ money.
5. I need money to _____ a car.

Dictionary

again _____	every _____
already _____	feed _____
always _____	late _____
angry _____	never _____
by _____	relax _____
crowded _____	slow _____
early _____	sometimes _____
elevator _____	

Practice B

Answer the questions about the photo story.

1. When does she get up?

   _____

2. How does she get to work?

   _____

3. How long does it take?

   _____

4. Why does she buy a cup of coffee?

   _____

5. Why is Mr. Davis angry?

   _____

6. How does she feel after work?

   _____

7. Why does she go for a walk in the park?

   _____

Practice D

1. What time do you usually get up on Mondays?

   _____

2. How do you get to work / school?

   _____

3. How long does it take you to get to work /
   school?

   _____

4. Are you sometimes late for class?

   _____

5. Do you drink coffee when you are tired?

   _____

6. How do you like your coffee? Black or regular?

   _____

7. What do you do to relax?

   _____

Could you help me?

A

★ How much are those radio batteries?
○ They're a dollar nineteen each.
★ Can you give me two, please?

B

★ Can you pass me the salt, please?
○ Here you are.
★ Thanks.

C

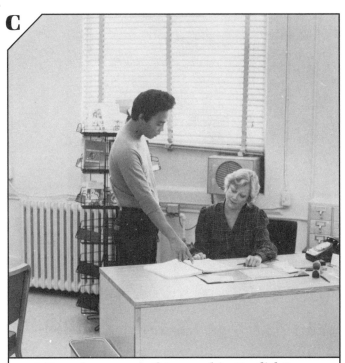

★ How do you say this word in English?
○ Garage.
★ Could you repeat that, please?
○ Garage.
★ Thank you.

D

★ Could you help me, please? This suitcase is very heavy.
○ Certainly.
★ Thank you. Take it to my car and put it in the trunk, please.

☞ Can you $\boxed{\text{verb}}$ . . . ?   Could you $\boxed{\text{verb}}$ . . . ?

Dictionary

battery _____	give _____	put _____	suitcase _____
certainly _____	heavy _____	repeat _____	trunk _____
each _____	pass _____	say _____	

Practice A

A. ★ How much _____ _____ radio batteries?

　○ They're a dollar nineteen _____ .

　★ Can you _____ _____ two, please?

B. ★ Can you _____ _____ the salt, please?

　○ Here you _____ .

　★ Thanks.

C. ★ How do you _____ this word in English?

　○ Garage.

　★ _____ you _____ that, please?

　○ Garage.

　★ Thank you.

D. ★ _____ you _____ me, please? This suitcase is very _____ .

　○ Certainly.

　★ Thank you. _____ it to my car and _____ it in the trunk, please.

Practice D

Write these conversations on a piece of paper.

1. pen / other
   ★ *Can you give me that pen, please?*
   ○ *This one?*
   ★ *No, the other one.*
2. book / black
3. apple / big
4. chair / new
5. _____ / _____

Practice B

☞ that book   those books

Write these conversations on a piece of paper.

1. cheese / $3.95/lb / two
   ★ *How much is that cheese?*
   ○ *$3.95 a pound.*
   ★ *Can you give me two pounds, please?*
2. oranges / 25¢ each / six
3. cake / $1.20 a piece / four
4. chocolates / 50¢ each / one
5. _____ / _____ / _____

Practice C

Write these conversations on a piece of paper.

1. address / 21 Main St. Apt #12
   ★ *What's your address?*
   ○ *Twenty-one Main Street, apartment twelve.*
   ★ *Could you repeat that, please?*
   ○ *Twenty-one Main Street, apartment twelve.*
2. telephone number / 936-8459
3. date of birth / July 9, 1948
4. last name / Santos
5. _____ / _____

Practice E

pass, pay, sign, speak, spell, take, use

1. Could you _*take*_ this suitcase to the car, please?
2. Could you _____ slowly, please? I don't understand.
3. Could you _____ here, please?
4. Could you _____ me the butter, please?
5. Can you _____ your first name, please?
6. Can you _____ the cashier, please?
7. Can you _____ that machine, please? This one doesn't work.

Apartment for rent.

"Hello. I'm calling about the apartment for rent."

"Yes, it's still available."

"Can you tell me about it, please?"

① ②

Yes, it's in a nice building in a quiet neighborhood. The apartment has a sunny living room with a dining room next to it.

③

There are two bedrooms.

④

The kitchen is large with a new stove and refrigerator.

⑤

There is a bathtub with a shower in the bathroom.

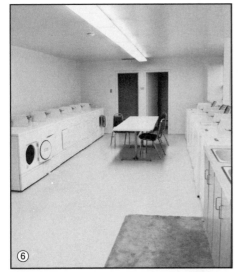

⑥

⑦

"How much is the rent?"

"Six hundred dollars a month."

"Sorry, that's too expensive for me."

In the basement of the building there is a laundry room with washers and dryers, and there is a parking garage for your car.

Dictionary

available _____	dryer _____	quiet _____	still _____
basement _____	neighborhood _____	rent _____	sunny _____
call _____	noisy _____	shower _____	tell _____

Practice A

★ Hello. I'm _____ about the apartment for _____ .

○ Yes, it's still _____ .

★ Can you _____ _____ about it, please?

○ Yes, it's in a nice building in a quiet _____ .

The apartment _____ a sunny living room with a _____ next to it. There _____ two bedrooms.

The _____ is large with a new _____ and refrigerator.

_____ is a bathtub with a shower in the bathroom.

In the _____ of the building there _____ a laundry room with washers and dryers, and _____ _____ a parking garage for your car.

★ How much is _____ _____ ?

○ Six hundred dollars a _____ .

★ Sorry, that's too _____ for me.

Practice B

★ What's your neighborhood like?
○ It's very noisy.

★ What's your apartment like?
○ It's small, but very sunny.

Answer these questions about the photo story.

1. What's the neighborhood like?

   _____

2. What's the living room like?

   _____

3. How many bedrooms are there?

   _____

4. Where is the dining room?

   _____

5. How much is the rent?

   _____

Practice C

1. *When is the apartment available* _____ ?
   The apartment is available now.

2. _____ ?
   There are two bedrooms.

3. _____ ?
   It's three hundred and fifty a month.

4. _____ ?
   The apartment is on the second floor.

5. _____ ?
   The neighborhood is very quiet.

6. _____ ?
   Yes, there is a parking garage.

7. _____ ?
   Yes, there is a laundry room.

8. _____ ?
   Yes, there is a shower in the bathroom.

9. _____ ?
   Yes, the apartment is near the subway.

Practice D

1. Tell me about your house or apartment.
   It _____ neighborhood.
   There _____ bedroom(s).
   The kitchen _____ .
   There _____ .

2. Do you live near a park? _____ .

3. Is there a supermarket in your neighborhood?
   _____ .

4. What else is in your neighborhood?
   _____ .

It's over there.

Where is the sugar?

It's over there on the counter.

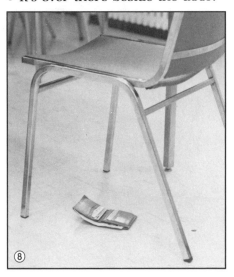

★ Where is the cream?
○ It's behind the napkins.

★ Where are the spoons?
○ They're in the tray.

★ Where is the garbage can?
○ It's in the corner.

★ Where is the telephone?
○ It's over there beside the door.

★ Where is the salt?
○ It's on the table in front of the menu.

★ Where are the restrooms?
○ They're downstairs, at the back.

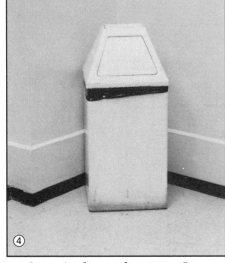

★ I can't find my wallet!
○ It's on the floor under the chair.

23

☞ beside = next to

Dictionary

behind _____   in front of _____   at the back _____   napkin _____

beside _____   on _____   downstairs _____   restroom _____

in _____   under _____   find _____   wallet _____

Practice A

1. ★ _____ _____ the sugar?
   ○ It's _____ there _____ the counter.

2. ★ _____ _____ the cream?
   ○ It's _____ the napkins.

3. ★ _____ _____ the spoons?
   ○ They're _____ the tray.

4. ★ _____ _____ the garbage can?
   ○ It's _____ the corner.

5. ★ _____ _____ the telephone?
   ○ It's _____ there _____ the door.

6. ★ _____ _____ the salt?
   ○ It's _____ the table in _____ of the menu.

7. ★ _____ _____ the restrooms?
   ○ They're _____ , at the back.

8. ★ I can't _____ my wallet!
   ○ It's _____ the floor _____ the chair.

Practice B

☞ this book   these books.

★ Can you help me, please?
○ Sure.

1. clothes / [washer] / basement
   Put these clothes in the washer in the basement.

2. flowers / [table] / dining room
   _____

3. plant / [TV] / living room
   _____

4. shoes / [bed] / John's bedroom
   _____

5. chair / [desk] / office
   _____

6. batteries / [radio] / over there
   _____

7. book / [telephone] / [table]
   _____

8. spoons / [tray] / [counter]
   _____

9. bicycle / [door] / garage
   _____

10. cream / [refrigerator]
    _____

11. gloves / [seat] / car

Practice C

(i) about, at, in, of, near

1. The train leaves _in_ half an hour.

2. The supermarket is _____ two blocks up the street.

3. Most _____ my friends live in California.

4. They study _____ the university.

5. She usually gets up _____ seven o'clock.

6. They live _____ a big park.

7. My house is _____ a very nice neighborhood.

(ii) to, too, two

1. Can I have _____ tickets, please?

2. Go _____ room number five.

3. I like _____ play cards.

4. She's a nurse and her sister is, _____ .

(iii) their, there, they're

1. _____ children study at the university.

2. _____ students at the university.

3. _____ is a laundry room in the basement.

4. It's over _____ beside the door.

Can you get me . . . ?

☞ get me
give me

Dictionary

above _____   right _____
below _____   shelf _____
look _____   sofa _____
newspaper _____   teapot _____

Practice A

★ Paul, _____ me the sugar, please.

○ Where is _____ ?

★ I think it's _____ the cupboard over

_____ .

○ It's _____ here.

★ _____ in the paper bag _____ the
teapot.

○ Oh, you're _____ . It's _____ .

★ Thanks. Can you _____ _____ the
butter, too?

○ _____ it in the refrigerator?

★ Yes. It's _____ the shelf _____ the
eggs.

○ _____ you are.

★ Thanks.

Practice B

☞ Where is <u>it</u>?   Where are <u>they</u>?

Write these conversations on a piece of paper.

1. newspaper / living room / dining room / [box] the
   table
   ★ *Can you get me the newspaper please?*
   ○ *Where is it?*
   ★ *I think it's in the living room.*
   ○ *It's not here.*
   ★ *Look in the dining room on the table.*
   ○ *You're right. It's here.*

2. my gloves / living room / bedroom / [box] my
   bag

3. my shoes / bedroom / living room / [box] the
   sofa

4. garbage can / basement / garage / [box] the
   door

5. my jacket / bedroom / laundry room / [box]
   the washer

6. car keys / car / living room / [box] the TV

7. sugar / cupboard / on the shelf below the cups

8. milk / refrigerator / on the shelf above the
   cheese

Practice C

1. *Where is he from* _____ ?
   I think he's from Hong Kong.

2. _____ ?
   I think Maria has three children.

3. _____ ?
   I think Donna is twenty-seven.

4. _____ ?
   I think Pat is a mechanic.

5. _____ ?
   I think the class starts at quarter after two.

6. _____ ?
   I think the drugstore is on the next corner.

7. _____ ?
   I think the rooms are downstairs.

8. _____ ?
   I think the park is two blocks from here.

9. _____ ?
   I think the bus leaves in half an hour.

10. _____ ?
    I think the rent is $300 a month.

11. _____ ?
    The airport? I think you take bus number 6.

REVIEW/Lessons 7–12

WHERE IS IT?

1. TRUE   FALSE
2. TRUE   FALSE
3. TRUE   FALSE
4. TRUE   FALSE
5. TRUE   FALSE
6. TRUE   FALSE

ANSWER THE QUESTIONS.

1. What time does John get up? _____
2. What does he usually have for breakfast? _____
3. How does he get to work? _____
4. What time does he start work? _____
5. Does he have a half hour for lunch? _____
6. How many hours does he work? _____
7. Where does he sometimes eat lunch? _____
8. Where does he always eat dinner? _____
9. What does he do after dinner? _____
10. How long does he sleep? _____

MAKE A SENTENCE.

1. an hour / much / How / you / make / do ?

   _____

2. to / It's / bed / to go / time .

   _____

3. How / the rent / much / is?

   _____

4. your / like / apartment / What's ?

   _____

5. Could / it / you / on / put / the table?

   _____

6. jacket / new / I / find / can't / my .

   _____

7. How / this / you / word / do / say / in English?

   _____

8. me / expensive / too / That's / for .

   _____

DISCOVER/Lessons 7–12

Discover A

KITCHEN
1. sink
2. pot
3. toaster
4. blender
5. counter
6. stove
7. dishwasher

LIVING ROOM
1. picture
2. armchair
3. stereo
4. carpet
5. sofa
6. coffee table
7. curtains

BEDROOM
1. closet
2. alarm clock
3. pillows
4. night table
5. blanket
6. dresser
7. bed

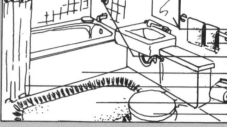

BATHROOM
1. mirror
2. towels
3. shower
4. bathtub
5. shower curtain
6. rug
7. toilet

1. Tell me about the kitchen.

a. There is a _dishwasher_ beside the refrigerator.

b. There are two _____ on the stove.

c. There is a _____ and a _____ on the counter.

d. There _____ .

2. Tell me about the living room.

a. There _____ a _____ beside the bookcase on the left.

b. There _____ a coffee table _____ the sofa.

c. There _____ an _____ beside the bookcase on the right.

d. There _____ .

3. Tell me about the bedroom.

a. There _____ two _____ on the bed.

b. There _____ an _____ on the night table.

c. There _____ a dresser _____ the closet.

d. There _____ .

4. Tell me about the bathroom.

a. There _____ a sink between the _____ and the _____ .

b. There _____ a _____ above the sink.

c. There _____ two _____ beside the sink on the right.

d. There _____ .

Discover B

★ I'm moving into my new apartment. Can you help me?

○ Sure. What can I do?

1. ★ Put the sofa in front of the window.
2. ★ Put the carpet on the floor in front of the sofa.
3. ★ Put the plant beside the sofa on the left.
4. ★ Put the small table against the wall across from the sofa.
5. ★ Put the TV on the table.
6. ★ Put the bookcase against the wall across from the door.
7. ★ Put the armchair in the right corner.

I want to . . . .

A

★ Are you tired?

○ Yes, I want to go home.

B

★ Dad, I'm bored.

○ Well, what do you want to do?

★ I want to play tennis.

C

★ Why do you want to buy a car?

○ Because I don't want to take the subway to work.

D

Jim is a dreamer. He wants to be rich. He wants to have a million dollars and to go to Hawaii. But, he doesn't want to work.

I	he	I	He
👉 Do you want to [verb] ...?	Does she want to [verb] ...?	You don't want to [verb]	She doesn't want to [verb] ....
we	it	We	It
they		They	

Dictionary

bored _____   million _____

Practice A

A. ★ _____ you tired?

○ Yes, I want _____ _____ home.

B. ★ Dad, I'm bored.

○ Well, what do you want _____ _____ ?

★ I want _____ _____ tennis.

C. ★ Why _____ _____ want to buy a car?

○ Because I _____ want to take the subway to work.

D. Jim _____ a dreamer. He wants _____ _____ rich.

He wants _____ _____ a million dollars and _____ _____ to Hawaii.

But, he _____ want to work.

Practice B

1. In photo A, why does she want to go home?

_____.

2. In photo B, why does he want to play tennis?

_____.

3. In photo C, what does he want to buy?

_____.

4. Why does he want to buy a car?

_____.

5. In photo D, what does Jim want to be?

_____.

6. How much money does Jim want to have?

_____.

7. Where does he want to go?

_____.

👉 This check is for you.

What do you want to buy? _____
Where do you want to go? _____
What do you want to do? _____

Practice C

Where?   What time?   What?

1. *Where do you want to go* _____ ?
   I want to go to the park.

2. _____ ?
   Jim wants to go to Hawaii.

3. _____ ?
   I want to eat dinner at eight o'clock.

4. _____ ?
   Tom wants to leave at six o'clock.

5. _____ ?
   They want to watch "Police Story."

6. _____ ?
   Linda wants to drink a glass of cold water.

Practice D

Write these conversations on a piece of paper.

1. he / buy a car / take the subway
   ★ *Why does he want to buy a car?*
   ○ *Because he doesn't want to take the subway.*

2. they / buy a house / live in an apartment

3. he / have a million dollars / work

4. she / buy a washer / go to the laundromat

5. you / take a taxi / be late

6. he / go to the restaurant / cook dinner

Where are you going?

A. ★ Where's George?
  ○ He's outside.
  ★ What's he doing?
  ○ He's fixing his motorcycle.

B. ★ Where are Ken and Susan?
  ○ They're at John's house.
  ★ What are they doing?
  ○ They're playing cards.

👉 Where is ║▶ Where's

I am	verb +ing.... (now)		

He
She is verb +ing.... (now)
It

he
Is she verb +ing...?
it

We
You are verb +ing.... (now)
They

we
Are you verb +ing...?
they

Dictionary

busy _____   light _____
fix _____   talk _____
letter _____

Practice A

★ Hey, Pat! Where _____ you _____ ?

○ I'm _____ downtown. _____ you

  want to _____ ?

★ I can't. I'm _____ .

○ What _____ you _____ ?

★ I'm _____ the light on my motorcycle.

A. ★ _____ George?

  ○ He's outside.

  ★ _____ _____ doing?

  ○ _____ fixing his motorcycle.

B. ★ Where _____ Ken and Susan?

  ○ _____ at John's house.

  ★ What _____ _____ doing?

  ○ They're _____ cards.

Practice B

1. ★ Where _is_ Tom going?
   ○ _He's_ going downtown.

2. ★ What _____ Lisa doing?
   ○ _____ writing a letter.

3. ★ Where _____ the children going?
   ○ _____ going downtown.

4. ★ What _____ the students reading?
   ○ _____ reading their English books.

5. ★ What _____ you drinking?
   ○ _____ drinking tea.

6. ★ _____ you and your husband going home?
   ○ No, _____ going to my mother's house.

7. ★ _____ David working in the garage?
   ○ No, _____ working in the basement.

Practice C

👉 write — writing   take — taking

Write these conversations on a piece of paper.

1. park / fix my car
   ★ _Where are you going?_
   ○ _I'm going to the park. Do you want to come?_
   ★ _I can't. I'm busy._
   ○ _What are you doing?_
   ★ _I'm fixing my car._

2. restaurant / study English
3. John's house / do the laundry
4. supermarket /cook dinner
5. library / write a letter
6. for a walk / take some photos
7. downtown / wash the kitchen floor

Practice D

👉 She's at home.   She's at the library.
   at school   at the supermarket
   at work   at the restaurant

Write these conversations on a piece of paper.

1. Maria / living room / talk on the telephone
   ★ _Where is Maria?_
   ○ _She's in the living room._
   ★ _What is she doing?_
   ○ _She's talking on the telephone._

2. Mr. Benson / school / teach the English class
3. Lisa / library / listen to an English cassette
4. the children / kitchen / eat breakfast
5. you / bedroom / read a book
6. your mother / supermarket / buy food for dinner
7. your parents / home / watch TV

What are you doing?

Plug in the vacuum cleaner and clean the carpet.

Unplug the vacuum cleaner and put it in the closet.

Put the dishes in the sink and turn on the water.

Turn off the water and wash the dishes. Be careful! Don't break them.

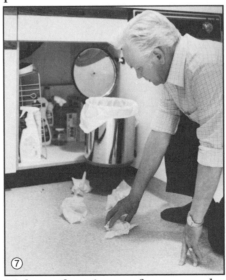

Pick up the pieces of paper and put them in the garbage can. Then, take out the garbage.

Open the window and let in some fresh air. Don't forget to close it later.

33

☞ Turn on/off the water.
           TV.
           radio.
           light.

Open/close the window.
           door.

Dictionary

break _____
careful _____
clean _____

fresh air _____
let _____
close _____

dark _____
forget _____
pick up _____

surprise _____
take out _____

Practice A

★ What _____ _____ doing?

○ What _____ _____ think? I'm
_____ the house.

★ Well, do you _____ any help?

○ What a _____ ! Sure, you _____ help.

○ Plug _____ the vacuum cleaner and
_____ the carpet.
_____ the vacuum cleaner and _____
it in the closet.
_____ the dishes in the sink and turn
_____ the water.
Turn _____ the water and _____ the
dishes. Be _____ ! Don't _____ them.
_____ _____ the pieces of paper and
put _____ in the garbage can. Then take
_____ the garbage.
_____ the window and _____ in
some fresh air. Don't _____ to close
it later.

Practice B

1. In photo #1, is he cleaning the house?
   No, he isn't _____ .

2. In photo #1, is she cleaning the carpet?
   _____ .

3. In photo #2, is she surprised?
   _____ .

4. In photo #3, is he washing the carpet?
   _____ .

5. In photo #4, is he plugging in the vacuum
   cleaner?
   _____ .

6. In photo #5, is he putting the dishes in the
   closet?
   _____ .

7. In photo #5, is he turning on the radio?
   _____ .

8. In photo #6, is he breaking the dishes?
   _____ .

9. In photo #7, is he picking up the pieces of
   paper?
   _____ .

10. In photo #8, is he closing the window?
    _____ .

Practice C

1. Are you studying English now? _Yes, I am_ .
2. Do you study English every evening? _____ .
3. Do you usually wash the dishes? _____ .
4. Are you washing the dishes now? _____ .
5. Do you eat breakfast in the morning? _____ .
6. Are you eating breakfast now? _____ .
7. Do you sometimes watch TV? _____ .
8. Are you watching TV now? _____ .
9. Are you cleaning the house now? _____ .
10. Do you clean the house every week? _____ .
11. Do you go to the park on Sundays? _____ .

Practice D

turn on, turn off, open, close, pick up, take out

1. It's dark. _____ the light.
2. _____ the radio. I don't like that
   program.
3. It's time to go to bed. _____ the TV.
4. _____ the pen. It's on the floor.
5. _____ the TV. I want to watch a movie.
6. _____ your book and read page ten.
7. _____ the door. It's cold outside.
8. Open the refrigerator, and _____ the
   milk.

How often do you . . . ?

A

★ Are you making dinner?

○ Yes, I am.

★ Do you usually make dinner?

○ Yes, I make dinner every day.

★ Every day! I never make dinner.

B

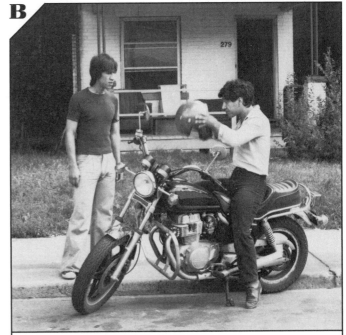

★ Hey, George! Where are you going?

○ I'm going to my sister's house.

★ How often do you visit your sister?

○ I visit her twice a month.

★ Well, have a nice time.

C

★ Are you waiting for the bus to Brookdale?

○ Yes, I am.

★ How often does the bus come?

○ It comes every twenty minutes.

D

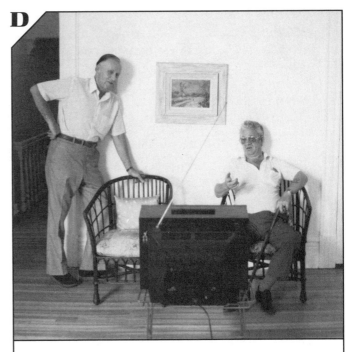

★ What are you watching?

○ I'm watching the football game.

★ Do you like football?

○ Yes, I watch it three times a week.

☞ I am watching TV. (now)
I watch TV. (every day, in the evening, usually . . .)

make dinner = cook dinner

Dictionary _____

How often . . . ? _____   twice _____
game _____   visit _____
once _____   wait _____

Practice A _____

A. ★ Are you _____ dinner?

○ Yes, I am.

★ Do you usually _____ dinner?

○ Yes, I _____ dinner every day.

★ Every day! I _____ make dinner.

B. ★ Hey, George! Where _____ _____ going?

○ I'm going to my _____ house.

★ How _____ do you _____ your sister?

○ I _____ _____ _____ twice a month.

★ Well, _____ a nice time.

C. ★ Are you _____ for the bus to Brookdale?

○ Yes, I am.

★ How _____ does the bus _____ ?

○ It _____ every twenty minutes.

D. ★ What _____ _____ watching?

○ I'm watching the football game.

★ _____ _____ like football?

○ Yes, I _____ it three _____ a week.

Practice B _____

Write these conversations on a piece of paper.

What?   Where?

1. do / watch the football game / twice a week
★ *What are you doing?*
○ *I'm watching the football game.*
★ *How often do you watch the football game?*
○ *I watch the football game twice a week.*
2. do / wash the dishes / once a day
3. go / the library / once a month
4. go / the dentist / once every six months
5. do / clean the house / once every two weeks
6. go / my English class / three times a week

Practice C _____

do, does, is, are

1. _____ you go to school every day?
2. _____ you making dinner?
3. _____ she using the new washer?
4. _____ they drinking orange juice or apple juice?
5. _____ they play cards every Thursday?
6. _____ he calling about the apartment?
7. _____ they speaking Chinese or Japanese?
8. _____ he usually drive to work?
9. _____ the class always start at one thirty?
10. _____ you studying English?

Practice D _____

☞ on Saturdays = every Saturday

1. I / wash   *I'm washing* _____ my car. *I wash* _____ my car once a week.
2. He / read   _____ the newspaper. _____ the newspaper every evening.
3. They / eat   _____ breakfast. They always _____ breakfast at 7:30.
4. She / work   _____ . She usually _____ on Saturdays.
5. I / study   _____ English. _____ English every day.
6. Jill / play   _____ tennis. _____ tennis every Saturday.

Would you like to . . . ?

★ Hello, Donna. This is Bill.
○ Oh, hi, Bill. How are you?
★ Not bad. Listen, what are you doing tonight?
○ Nothing.
★ Would you like to go to a movie?
○ Yes. That sounds good.
★ I'd like to see *The Temple of Doom* at the University Theater. Is that all right with you?
○ That's fine. When do you want to meet?
★ How about 7:30?
○ OK. Where do you want to meet?
★ Can we meet in front of the theater?
○ Sure. See you tonight.

Would you like to go to a movie?

Would you like to go to the zoo?

Would you like to go to the beach?

Would you like to go dancing?

Would you like to go swimming?

Would you like to go shopping?   **37**

☞ I would like ‖‖▶ I'd like

Practice A

★ Hello, Donna. _____ is Bill.

○ Oh, hi, Bill. _____ are you?

★ Not bad. Listen, what are you doing _____ ?

○ _____ .

★ _____ _____ like to go to a movie?

○ Yes. That sounds good.

★ _____ _____ to see *The Temple of Doom* at the University Theater. Is that all _____ with you?

○ That's fine. When _____ you want to meet?

★ How about 7:30?

○ OK. _____ do you _____ to meet?

★ _____ _____ meet in front of the theater?

○ Sure. See you tonight.

Would you like to . . . ?

1. *go to a movie* _____   4. _____
2. _____   5. _____
3. _____   6. _____

Dictionary

all right _____   something _____
not bad _____   theater _____
nothing _____   tonight _____

Practice B

Write these conversations on a piece of paper.

1. swimming / 4:00 / on the corner of Main and Bay St.
   ★ *Would you like to go swimming?*
   ○ *Sure. What time do you want to meet?*
   ★ *How about four o'clock?*
   ○ *That's fine. Where do you want to meet?*
   ★ *Can we meet on the corner of Main and Bay Street?*
   ○ *OK. See you later!*

2. dancing / 9:15 / at your house

3. the park / 2:30 / on the corner of King and West St.

4. a restaurant / 7:30 / at the Seaside Restaurant

5. shopping / 1:00 / in front of the supermarket

6. _____ / _____ / _____

Practice C

★ Would you like a sandwich?
○ No, thanks, but I'd like an ice cream cone.

★ Would you like some tea?
○ No, thanks, but I'd like some coffee.

Write these conversations on a piece of paper.

1. tea / coffee
   ★ *Would you like some tea?*
   ○ *No, thanks, but I'd like some coffee.*
2. apple / orange
3. bread / cake
4. salad / soup
5. banana / glass of water
6. _____ / _____

Practice D

★ Would you like something to drink?
○ Yes, I'd like a glass of water, please.

★ Would you like something to eat?
○ Yes, I'd like some soup, please.

Write these conversations on a piece of paper.

1. eat / salad
   ★ *Would you like something to eat?*
   ○ *I'd like some salad, please.*
2. drink / orange juice
3. eat / cheese
4. drink / cup of coffee
5. eat / chicken sandwich
6. _____ / _____

Which one is yours?

A

①

Whose pen is this?

It's not mine. I think it's hers.

②

Is this yours?

No, it's his.

③

B

Can you give me my jacket, please?

Which one is yours?

①

The blue one.

②

Here you are.

Thanks.

③

C

①

②

③

★ I'm looking for Mr. Thomson.

○ Oh, yes. He's over there. He's wearing the dark sunglasses.

★ Who's the woman in the white sweater?

○ That's Sandra King.

★ Who's Dan Wade?

○ He's the man wearing the black leather jacket.

39

Who is |||⟹ Who's

It's my pen.   → It's mine.
It's your pen. → It's yours.
It's his pen. → It's his.
It's her pen. → It's hers.

Dictionary

blue _____   sweater _____
leather _____   wear _____
sunglasses _____   whose _____

Practice A

A. ★ _____ pen is this?

○ It's not _____ . I think it's _____ .

★ Is this _____ ?

○ No, it's _____ .

B. ★ Can you _____ _____ my jacket, please?

○ _____ one is yours?

★ _____ blue one.

○ Here _____ are.

★ Thanks.

C. 1. ★ I'm _____ for Mr. Thomson.

○ Oh, yes. _____ over there. He's _____ the dark sunglasses.

2. ★ _____ the woman in the white sweater?

○ _____ Sandra King.

3. ★ _____ Dan Wade?

○ He's the man _____ the black leather jacket.

Practice B

Write these conversations on a piece of paper.

1. book / big / on the desk
   ★ *Can you give me my book, please?*
   ○ *Which one is yours?*
   ★ *The big one on the desk.*
2. pen / black / behind the telephone
3. dictionary / small / on the chair
4. pencil / blue / under the book
5. _____ / _____ / _____

Practice C

Write these conversations on a piece of paper.

1. Mrs. Taylor / white dress
   ★ *I'm looking for Mrs. Taylor.*
   ○ *She's over there. She's wearing the white dress.*
2. Susan Bennett / dark sunglasses
3. the supervisor / black jacket
4. Mr. Lee / blue sweater
5. _____ / _____

Practice D

Whose?   Who?   Which?   What?

1. *Whose radio is this?* _____ ?
   It's John's radio.

2. _____ ?
   I want the big apple.

3. _____ ?
   The black pen on the desk is mine.

4. _____ ?
   It's my pen.

5. _____ ?
   That's Jim Gibson over there.

6. _____ ?
   The woman wearing the blue dress is my sister.

Practice E

my, mine, your, yours, his, her, hers

1. Is that *your* husband? Yes, that's _____ husband.

2. Is this Maria's car? Yes, it's _____ .

3. Is this John's radio? Yes, it's _____ .

4. Is this your book? Yes, it's _____ .

5. Is this _____ ? Yes, it's my pen.

6. Is that your brother? Yes, that's _____ brother.

7. Is that Maria's boyfriend? Yes, that's _____ boyfriend.

8. Is that John's sister? Yes, that's _____ sister.

REVIEW/Lessons 13—18

WHICH ONE IS IT?

1. a. What's he doing?
   b. What's she doing?

2. a. Where do you want to go?
   b. Where do they want to go?

3. a. They're playing cards.
   b. They aren't playing cards.

4. a. When is she working?
   b. Where is she working?

5. a. Turn on the light.
   b. Turn off the light.

6. a. Put it on the table.
   b. Put them on the table.

7. a. Whose is this?
   b. Who's this?

8. a. Which one is yours?
   b. Which one is hers?

9. a. Would you like to go to a movie?
   b. Would she like to go to a movie?

WHAT'S THE ANSWER?

1. a. once a month
   b. twice a month

2. a. at 11:45
   b. at 11:55

3. a. Yes, he does.
   b. No, he doesn't.

4. a. Yes, they do.
   b. No, they don't.

5. a. Yes, they do.
   b. No, they don't.

6. a. Yes, they do.
   b. I don't know.

7. a. an American motorcycle
   b. a Japanese motorycle

8. a. Yes, I think so.
   b. No, I don't think so.

9. a. Yes, it is.
   b. I don't know.

10. a. Yes, he is.
    b. No, he isn't.

11. a. in the evening
    b. in the morning

12. a. No, they aren't.
    b. Yes, they are.

HOW ABOUT YOU?

1. Do you clean the house? _____

2. Are you cleaning the house now? _____

3. What do you do when you clean the house? _____

_____

4. Do you like to clean the house? _____

5. Are you studying English now? _____

6. Do you study English in the evening? _____

7. What other things do you do in the evening? _____

_____

8. Are you making dinner? _____

9. Do you usually make dinner? _____

DISCOVER/Lessons 13—18
Discover A

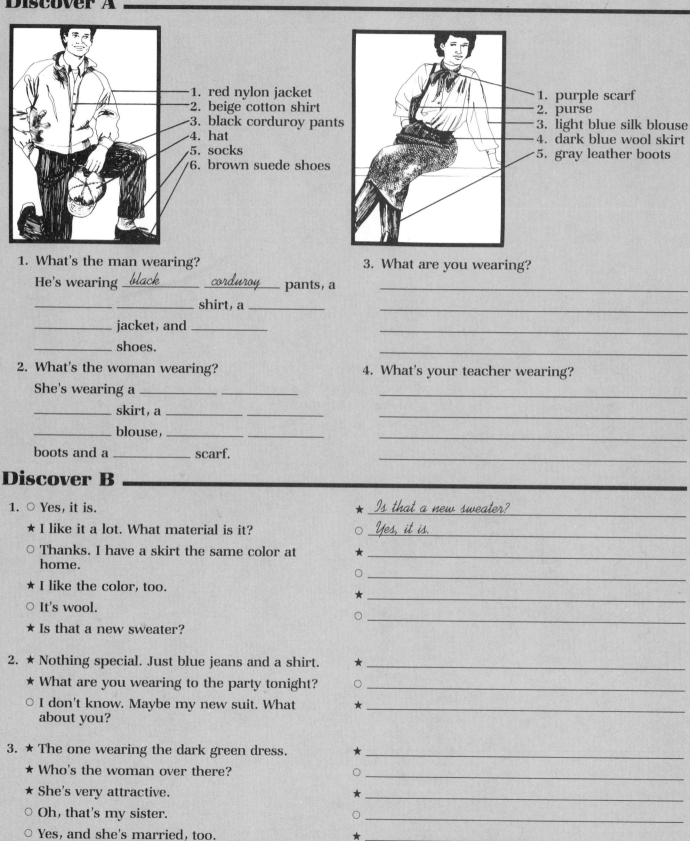

1. red nylon jacket
2. beige cotton shirt
3. black corduroy pants
4. hat
5. socks
6. brown suede shoes

1. purple scarf
2. purse
3. light blue silk blouse
4. dark blue wool skirt
5. gray leather boots

1. What's the man wearing?

   He's wearing _black_ _corduroy_ pants, a

   _____ _____ shirt, a _____

   _____ jacket, and _____

   _____ shoes.

2. What's the woman wearing?

   She's wearing a _____ _____

   _____ skirt, a _____ _____

   _____ blouse, _____ _____

   boots and a _____ scarf.

3. What are you wearing?

   _____

   _____

   _____

   _____

4. What's your teacher wearing?

   _____

   _____

   _____

   _____

   _____

Discover B

1. ○ Yes, it is.

   ★ I like it a lot. What material is it?

   ○ Thanks. I have a skirt the same color at home.

   ★ I like the color, too.

   ○ It's wool.

   ★ Is that a new sweater?

   ★ _Is that a new sweater?_ _____

   ○ _Yes, it is._ _____

   ★ _____

   ○ _____

   ★ _____

   ○ _____

2. ★ Nothing special. Just blue jeans and a shirt.

   ★ What are you wearing to the party tonight?

   ○ I don't know. Maybe my new suit. What about you?

   ★ _____

   ○ _____

   ★ _____

3. ★ The one wearing the dark green dress.

   ★ Who's the woman over there?

   ★ She's very attractive.

   ○ Oh, that's my sister.

   ○ Yes, and she's married, too.

   ○ Which one?

   ★ _____

   ○ _____

   ★ _____

   ○ _____

   ★ _____

   ○ _____

I'd like to apply for a job.

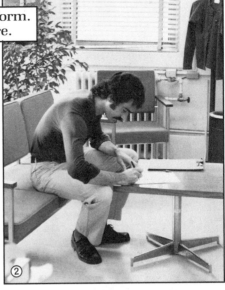

Give this form to the secretary.
Give this book to the teacher.
Give this pen to the student.

Give <u>something</u> to <u>somebody</u>.

Dictionary

apply _____   form _____
appointment _____   hall _____
come back _____   manager _____
fill out _____   somebody _____

Practice A

★ I'd like _____ _____ for a job.

○ Please _____ _____ this application

form. You can _____ the table over there.

★ I'm _____ .

○ OK. _____ this form _____ the

secretary in room four and _____ for Mr.
Badali. He's the manager.

★ Where's room four?

○ _____ _____ the hall. It's the second

room _____ the right.

· · · · · · · · · · · ·

■ I'm sorry. Mr. Badali is _____ now. Can

you _____ _____ in an hour?

★ Yes, I _____ .

■ Good. I'll make an _____ for you.

Practice B

Give this book to Tony.   → Give <u>it</u> to <u>him</u>.
Give these books to Maria.   → Give <u>them</u> to <u>her</u>.
Give the pen to Tony and me.   → Give <u>it</u> to <u>us</u>.
Give the key to Maria and Tony.→ Give <u>it</u> to <u>them</u>.

1. Give the jacket to Susan. *Give it to her* .

2. Give this cake to the children. _____ .

3. Give these pens to Mr. Benson. _____ .

4. Give the money to John and me. _____ .

5. Give the stamp to your mother. _____ .

6. Give this photo to Ken. _____ .

7. Give those sandwiches to Lisa and me. _____

_____ .

8. Give the keys to your sister. _____ .

Practice C

Write these conversations on a piece of paper.

1. form / secretary / room 10 / 2nd / right
   ★ *Give this form to the secretary in room ten.*
   ○ *Where's room ten?*
   ★ *Go down the hall. It's the second room on the right.*

2. money / cashier / room 1 / 1st / left

3. book / teacher / room 15 / 3rd / left

4. _____ / _____ / _____ / _____ / _____

Practice D

Write these conversations on a piece of paper.

1. dictionary / student in the blue dress / Maria
   ★ *Give this dictionary to the student in the blue dress.*
   ○ *What's her name?*
   ★ *Maria.*

2. jacket / man in the white shirt / Mr. Davis

3. suitcase / woman in the green sweater / Ms. Wilson

4. _____ / _____ / _____

Can you start next Monday?

1. Hello. I have an appointment with Mr. Badali at three o'clock.
Yes, you can go in now. Mr. Badali is expecting you.

2. Hello. I'm Tony Santos.
Come in, Mr. Santos. Sit down.

3. So, you are a mechanic. How many years experience do you have?
Five years.

4. Do you have a mechanic's license?
Yes, I do.
Can you repair trucks?
Yes, I can.

5. Good. We need somebody to take care of our trucks, but you have to work on Saturdays.
That's fine with me.

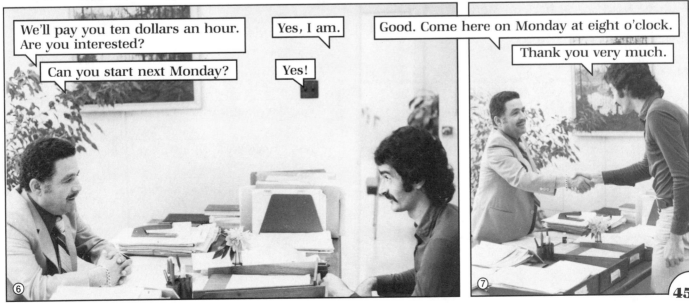

6. We'll pay you ten dollars an hour. Are you interested?
Yes, I am.
Can you start next Monday?
Yes!

7. Good. Come here on Monday at eight o'clock.
Thank you very much.

45

☞ we will ‖‖⇒ we'll

Dictionary

expect _____   have to _____   license _____   take care _____
experience _____   interested _____   repair _____   truck _____

Practice A

★ Hello. I have an appointment _____ Mr. Badali at three o'clock.

○ Yes, you can _____ _____ now. Mr. Badali is expecting you.

★ Hello. I'm Tony Santos.

■ Come _____ , Mr. Santos. Sit _____ .

■ So, you are a mechanic. How _____ _____ experience do you have?

★ Five years.

■ _____ _____ have a mechanic's license?

★ Yes, I _____ .

■ _____ _____ repair trucks?

★ Yes, I _____ .

■ Good. We need _____ to take care of our trucks, but you _____ _____ work on Saturdays.

★ That's fine with me.

■ We'll _____ you ten dollars an hour. _____ _____ interested?

★ Yes, I _____ .

■ _____ _____ start next Monday?

★ Yes!

■ Good. _____ here on Monday at eight o'clock.

★ Thank you _____ _____ .

Practice D

1. Can you drive a car? _____
2. Can you repair a car? _____
3. Tell me something you can do very well.
   _____
4. Tell me something you can't do.
   _____
5. What's your father's occupation?
   _____
6. How many years experience does he have?
   _____

Practice B

Write these conversations on a piece of paper.

1. cook / five / $300 a week / Monday
   ★ *What's your occupation?*
   ○ *I'm a cook.*
   ★ *How many years experience do you have?*
   ○ *Five years.*
   ★ *We'll pay you $300 a week. Are you interested?*
   ○ *Yes, I am.*
   ★ *Can you start on Monday?*
   ○ *Yes, I can.*

2. cashier / two / $4 an hour / tonight
3. secretary / four / $250 a week / tomorrow
4. truck driver / fifteen / $10.50 an hour / next Tuesday

Practice C

Do you?   Are you?   Can you?

1. *Can you drive a car* _____ ?
   Yes, I can drive a car.

2. _____ ?
   Yes, I have a car.

3. _____ ?
   No, I can't work on Saturdays.

4. _____ ?
   No, I'm not a mechanic.

5. _____ ?
   Yes, I am a student.

6. _____ ?
   Yes, we need a mechanic to repair our trucks.

7. _____ ?
   Yes, I have an appointment at 3:00.

8. _____ ?
   No, I can't start next Monday.

9. _____ ?
   Yes, I am interested in this job.

10. _____ ?
    Yes, I can speak Spanish.

46

When will he be home?

A

★ Hello, is Jim there?

○ Sorry, you have the wrong number.

★ Oh, I'm sorry.

. . . .

★ Hello, can I speak to Jim, please?

■ Jim isn't home.

★ When will he be home?

■ He'll be home tonight. Can I take a message?

★ Yes, please tell him to call Lisa at 943-7551.

■ OK. Bye.

B

★ Hello. I'd like to make an appointment with Dr. West for tomorrow morning.

○ I'm sorry. Dr. West won't be in until next week.

★ Will she be in on Tuesday?

○ Yes, she will.

★ Could I make an appointment for Tuesday at 3:00?

○ Yes, that's fine. And your name, please?

★ Jean Wyman.

○ Could you spell your last name, please?

★ W-Y-M-A-N.

C

★ Hello, operator, I want to call collect to Boston.

○ Please dial zero, the area code and then the number. Tell the operator it's a collect call.

. . . .

★ Hello, operator, I want to call collect to Mr. John Davis, and my name is Frank Rico.

○ I'm sorry. The line is busy.

★ OK, I'll try again later.

. . . .

○ Hello. Mr. John Davis, please.

■ Speaking.

○ I have a collect call from Mr. Rico in Miami. Will you accept the call?

■ No, I won't.

☞ will not ⫸ won't

Dictionary

accept _____   collect call _____   message _____   wrong _____
area code _____   dial _____   until _____

Practice A

A. ★ Hello, is Jim _____ ?

   ○ Sorry, you have the _____ _____ .

   ★ Oh, I'm sorry.

   · · · · · · · · · · · ·

   ★ Hello, can I _____ to Jim, please?

   ■ Jim isn't _____ .

   ★ When _____ he be home?

   ■ _____ be home tonight. Can I take a _____ ?

   ★ Yes, please _____ him to call Lisa at 943-7551.

   ■ OK. Bye.

B. ★ Hello. I'd like _____ _____ an appointment with Dr. West for _____ morning.

   ○ I'm sorry. Dr. West _____ be in until next week.

   ★ _____ she be in on Tuesday?

   ○ Yes, she _____ .

   ★ _____ I make an appointment for Tuesday at 3:00?

   ○ Yes, that's _____ . And your name, please?

   ★ Jean Wyman.

   ○ Could you _____ your last name, please?

   ★ W-Y-M-A-N.

C. ★ Hello, operator, I want _____ _____ collect to Boston.

   ○ Please _____ zero, the _____ code and then the number. _____ the operator it's a collect call.

   · · · · · · · · · · · ·

   ★ Hello, operator, I want _____ _____ collect to Mr. John Davis, and my name is Frank Rico.

   ○ I'm sorry. The _____ is busy.

   ★ OK, I'll _____ again later.

   · · · · · · · · · · · ·

   ○ Hello. Mr. John Davis, please.

   ■ _____ .

   ○ I have a collect call _____ Mr. Rico in Miami. _____ you accept the call?

   ■ No, I _____ .

| **Future:** tonight, tomorrow | | | |
| next week, next month, next _____ | | | |
in an hour, in two days, in _____			
I will	I'll	I	I
You will	You'll	you	You
He will	He'll	he	He
She will ⫸	She'll	Will she [verb]...?	She won't [verb]....
It will	It'll	it	It
We will	We'll	we	We
They will	They'll	they	They

Practice B

Write these conversations on a piece of paper.

1. Maria / next Friday
   ★ *When will Maria be home?*
   ○ *She'll be home next Friday.*
2. the children / later
3. Mr. Davis / tonight
4. you / in two hours
5. you and Tom / next week
6. your mother / in about ten minutes

Practice C

Write these conversations on a piece of paper.

1. Dr. West / 3:00 / 4:00
   ★ *Will Doctor West be in at three o'clock?*
   ○ *No, she won't be in until four.*
2. Mr. Davis / tomorrow / next Friday
3. you / early this evening / late tonight
4. students / this afternoon / tomorrow morning
5. the dentist / next week / next month
6. you and your husband / 6:00 / 8:00

I have to . . . .

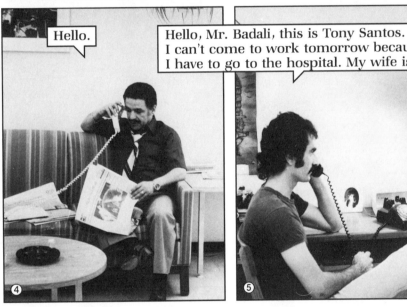

☞ Can I ⬚verb⬚...?
May I ⬚verb⬚...?

I have to ⬚verb⬚....

Dictionary

hear _____   soon _____

Practice A

★ Hello. _____ I speak to Mr. Badali, please?

○ _____ calling, please?

★ Tony Santos.

○ OK, just a _____ . I'll _____ him.

○ Jack, it's _____ _____ .

■ Hello.

★ Hello, Mr. Badali. This is Tony Santos. I

_____ come to work tomorrow because I

_____ _____ go to the hospital. My

wife is sick.

■ I'm sorry to _____ that. I hope she

_____ better soon.

★ Thank you. I hope so, too. _____

_____ at work the day after tomorrow.

■ That's fine, Tony. Good-bye.

Practice B

ask, call, get, tell, help

1. ★ Please tell John to call me.
   ○ OK, *I'll tell him* .

2. ★ What's Maria's last name?
   ○ I don't know. *I'll ask her* .

3. ★ Can you get me the milk?
   ○ OK, _____ .

4. ★ Please help Lisa wash the dishes.
   ○ OK, _____ .

5. ★ Can you help me, please?
   ○ OK, _____ .

6. ★ Please tell your father to come downstairs.
   ○ OK, _____ .

7. ★ Where do they live?
   ○ I don't know. _____ .

8. ★ Can you get my shoes?
   ○ OK, _____ .

9. ★ Could you call us tonight?
   ○ _____ .

10. ★ Is he married?
    ○ I don't know. _____ .

Practice C

Write these conversations on a piece of paper.

1. come to dinner next Friday / work
   ★ *I can't come to dinner next Friday.*
   ○ *Why not?*
   ★ *Because I have to go to work.*

2. come to work tomorrow / go to the dentist
3. go to a movie tonight / do the laundry
4. go dancing with you / meet my boyfriend
5. go shopping / study English
6. help you now / make dinner
7. finish this now / go home
8. _____ / _____

Practice D

Write these conversations on a piece of paper.

1. work tomorrow / no
   ★ *Will you be at work tomorrow?*
   ○ *No, I won't be there.*

2. school the day after tomorrow / no
3. the dance tonight / yes
4. the library this afternoon / yes
5. home soon / no
6. the restaurant later / yes
7. _____ / _____

50

When can you do it?

A

★ Can you type this letter?

○ I can't right now. I'm too busy.

★ When can you do it?

○ I can do it tomorrow morning.

B

★ Can I borrow your dictionary for a couple
of minutes?

○ OK, but don't forget to give it back.

★ Don't worry. I won't forget.

C

★ Let's go to a movie.

○ I can't. I have a doctor's appointment.

★ What time do you have to be there?

○ I can't remember. Either 4:00 or 4:30.

D

★ Can Lisa go to the party tonight?

○ No, she can't. She has to stay home.

★ Why does she have to stay home?

○ Because her daughter is sick.

| I/You/We/They have to ⬚verb.... | Do you have to ⬚verb...? | I don't have to ⬚verb.... |
| He/She/It   has to ⬚verb.... | Does she have to ⬚verb...? | He doesn't have to ⬚verb.... |

Dictionary

a couple of _____   either _____   party _____   right now _____
borrow _____   let's = let us _____   remember _____   stay _____

Practice A

A. ★ _____ _____ type this letter?

○ I _____ right now. I'm too busy.

★ When can you _____ _____ ?

○ I _____ _____ _____
tomorrow morning.

B. ★ Can I _____ your dictionary for a
_____ of minutes?

○ OK, but _____ forget to give it _____ .

★ _____ worry. I _____ forget.

C. ★ _____ go to a movie.

○ I _____ . I have a doctor's
appointment.

★ What time do you _____ _____ be
there?

○ I can't _____ . Either four or four
thirty.

D. ★ Can Lisa go to the _____ tonight?

○ No, she can't. She _____ _____ stay home.

★ Why does she _____ _____ stay
home?

○ _____ her daughter is sick.

Practice B

Write these conversations on a piece of paper.

1. fix my car / tomorrow morning
   ★ *Can you fix my car?*
   ○ *I can't right now. I'm too busy.*
   ★ *When can you do it?*
   ○ *I can do it tomorrow morning.*

2. give this to Mr. Smith / this afternoon
3. take this to room ten / in half an hour
4. make dinner / later
5. wash the dishes / in a couple of minutes
6. _____ / _____

Practice C

Write these conversations on a piece of paper.

1. Lisa / go dancing / study English
   ★ *Can Lisa go dancing tonight?*
   ○ *No, she can't. She has to study English.*

2. Jeff and Nora / go to the party / work
3. Susan / go for a walk with us / do the laundry
4. You and Bill / go to a movie / clean our
   apartment
5. Mr. Benson / have dinner with us / meet
   somebody
6. The secretary / type this letter / go home
7. You / _____ / _____

Practice D

Where?   What time?   Why?   Who?

1. *Who do you have to meet* _____ ?
   I have to meet my sister.

2. _____ ?
   He has to go to school.

3. _____ ?
   They have to be there at three o'clock.

4. _____ ?
   I have to stay home because my wife is sick.

5. _____ ?
   My wife has to be at work at nine o'clock.

6. _____ ?
   He has to call Mr. Badali.

7. _____ ?
   I have to go to room ten.

8. _____ ?
   She has to sell her car because she needs the
   money.

You should . . . .

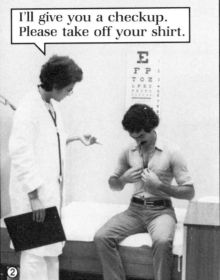

What's your problem Mr. Santos?

I'm always tired, doctor.

I'll give you a checkup. Please take off your shirt.

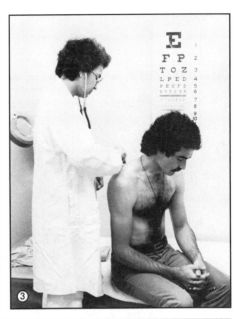

You can put on your shirt now.

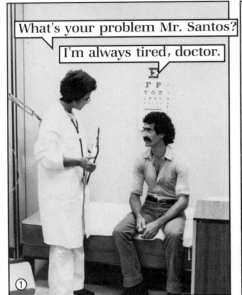

You seem healthy. Do you have any problems at home or at work?

Well, I worry a lot because I have a new job, and I have problems with English.

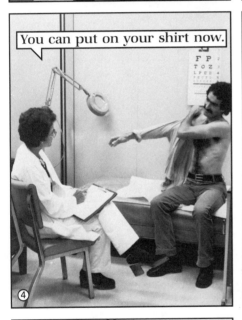

You shouldn't worry so much. You should try to relax. How long have you been in Canada?

A year and a half.

Is your family here?

My wife is, but all our friends are in Brazil.

Hmm, I think you need a vacation in Brazil, not a doctor.

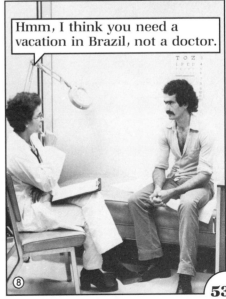

53

☞ You should boxed:verb ....   should not ➠ shouldn't

Dictionary

checkup _____   problem _____   seem _____   take off _____
healthy _____   put on _____   should _____   vacation _____

Practice A

★ What's your _____ Mr. Santos?

○ I'm _____ tired, doctor.

★ I'll give you a _____ .
Please _____ _____ your shirt.

· · · · · · · · · · · · · · ·

★ You can _____ _____ your shirt now.
You seem _____ . Do you have _____
problems at home or at work?

○ Well, I worry _____ _____ because I
have a new job, and I have problems with
English.

★ You _____ worry so much. You _____
try to relax. _____ _____ have you
been in Canada?

○ A year and _____ half.

★ _____ your family here?

○ My wife is, but all _____ friends are in
Brazil.

★ Hmm, I _____ you need a vacation in
Brazil, not a doctor.

Practice B

should   **shouldn't**

1. ★ I'm hungry.
   ○ You *should* *eat* a sandwich.
2. ★ I worry a lot.
   ○ You _____ _____ so much.
3. ★ I'm thirsty.
   ○ You _____ _____ something.
4. ★ I'm cold.
   ○ You _____ _____ on your sweater.
5. ★ I feel sick.
   ○ You _____ _____ so much ice cream.
6. ★ I'm tired.
   ○ You _____ _____ to bed so late.
7. ★ I'm hot.
   ○ You _____ _____ off your jacket.
8. ★ I'm bored.
   ○ You _____ _____ dancing.
9. ★ I need money.
   ○ You _____ _____ a job.
10. ★ My refrigerator isn't working.
    ○ You _____ _____ a new one.

Practice C

1. married / two years
   ★ *How long have you been married* ?
   ○ *Two years* .
2. in New York / three months
   ★ _____ ?
   ○ _____ .
3. a mechanic / ten years
   ★ _____ ?
   ○ _____ .
4. sick / five days
   ★ _____ ?
   ○ _____ .
5. in this English class / _____
   ★ _____ ?
   ○ _____ .

Practice D

☞ I like to boxed:verb ...   I can boxed:verb ...
I want to boxed:verb ...   I will boxed:verb ...
I have to boxed:verb ...   I should boxed:verb ...

**fill out, get off, make, meet, play, speak,
stay, take, visit**

1. He likes *to play* tennis on the weekends.
2. She can _____ English and Japanese.
3. She has _____ an application form.
4. You should _____ a taxi.
5. You have _____ at Bedford Road.
6. I will _____ an appointment for you.
7. They want _____ home tonight.
8. We like _____ our friends.
9. I can _____ you at the library at one o'clock.

REVIEW/Lessons 19—24

WHICH ONE IS IT?

1. a. Give this to the secretary
   b. Give these to the secretary

2. a. We'll pay you $250 a week.
   b. We'll pay you $215 a week.

3. a. Please dial 976-5430.
   b. Please dial 976-5340.

4. a. I won't accept the call.
   b. I want to accept the call.

5. a. You should eat a lot.
   b. You shouldn't eat a lot.

6. a. We have to go home.
   b. He has to go home.

7. a. I'll get him.
   b. I'll get them.

8. a. We'll be in later.
   b. He'll be in later.

9. a. He can drive a truck.
   b. He can't drive a truck.

YES OR NO?

1.	Is Maria a secretary?	YES	NO
2.	Does she have seven years experience?	YES	NO
3.	Can she type?	YES	NO
4.	Does she want this job?	YES	NO
5.	Will she start next Tuesday?	YES	NO
6.	Will she work in an office?	YES	NO
7.	Will she sell clothes?	YES	NO
8.	Will she answer the phone?	YES	NO
9.	Will she speak only Spanish?	YES	NO
10.	Will she work six days a week?	YES	NO

FINISH THE CONVERSATIONS WITH THE CORRECT FORM OF: do, does, is, are, can, will.

1. ★ _____ Maria going downtown?
   ○ No, she _____ going downtown.

2. ★ _____ Tom have to go to work?
   ○ No, he _____ have to go to work.

3. ★ _____ they eating dinner?
   ○ No, they _____ eating dinner.

4. ★ Excuse me. _____ you help me?
   ○ I'm sorry. I _____ help you. I'm busy.

5. ★ _____ the doctor be in tomorrow?
   ○ No, she _____ be in tomorrow.

6. ★ _____ John want to buy a new car?
   ○ No, he _____ want to buy a new car.

7. ★ _____ I borrow your dictionary, please?
   ○ No, you _____ borrow my dictionary.

8. ★ _____ your sister studying economics?
   ○ No, she _____ studying economics.

DISCOVER/Lessons 19–24
Discover A

★ Hello, Kathy. Are you coming to school today?
○ No, I don't feel well.
★ What's the matter?
○ I have a cold.
★ You should drink lots of liquids and go to bed.
.... (next day) ....
★ Hello, Kathy. How do you feel today?
○ I feel much better.
★ Will you be at school tomorrow?
○ Yes, I'll be there.
★ Good. I'll see you then.

1. a headache

2. an upset stomach

3. a cold

4. a toothache

5. a sore back

6. sore feet

Bend your knees when you lift heavy things. Rest and wear comfortable shoes. Take vitamin C and drink lots of liquids.	Call the dentist. Don't eat rich food. Lie down and relax.

1. ★ *What's the matter?*
   ○ *I have a headache.*
   ★ *You should lie down and relax.*

2. ★ *What's the matter?*
   ○ *I have an upset stomach.*
   ★ _____ .

3. ★ _____ ?
   ○ _____ .
   ★ _____ .

4. ★ _____ ?
   ○ _____ .
   ★ _____ .

5. ★ _____ ?
   ○ _____ .
   ★ _____ .

6. ★ _____ ?
   ○ _____ .
   ★ _____ .

Discover B

○ No, I'm not.
★ Why can't you sleep?
★ You look very tired.
★ Are you taking any medicine?
○ I know, doctor. I can't sleep.
○ For about a week.
○ Because I have a headache and my stomach is upset.
★ Take this prescription to the drugstore. They will give you some medicine for your problem.
★ How long have you been sick like this?

★ *You look very tired.*
○ _____
★ _____
○ _____
★ _____
○ _____
★ _____
○ _____
★ _____

What's the weather like?

A

1. It's sunny.

2. It's raining.

3. It's windy.

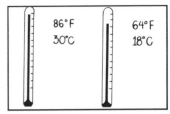

4. It's hot.   It's warm.

86°F 30°C   64°F 18°C

5. It's cloudy.

6. It's snowing.

7. It's foggy.

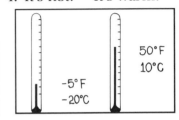

8. It's cold.   It's cool.

-5°F -20°C   50°F 10°C

B

① ★ What's the weather like today?
○ Beautiful. It's sunny and hot.

② ★ What's the weather like today?
○ Terrible! It's snowing and cold.

③ ★ What's the weather like today?
○ So-so. It's raining, but it's warm.

C

And now for the weather report. Yesterday was a cloudy and cool day with a low of 46 degrees. Today it's partly cloudy and windy with a chance of rain this evening. The temperature in downtown Boston right now is 50. The weather will change overnight, and tomorrow will be sunny with a high of 59.

Looking at the international weather, Moscow is minus 5 and cloudy. It's raining in Paris and the temperature there is 42 degrees. Rio de Janeiro is sunny with a temperature of 86. Those people in Rio are very lucky. That's it for today. I'll be back tomorrow at the same time.

is·····>was   (yesterday)   PAST
is·····>will be (tomorrow)   FUTURE

Dictionary

chance _____   international _____   overnight _____   report _____
change _____   low _____   partly _____   temperature _____
degrees _____   lucky _____   people _____   terrible _____
high _____   minus _____   plus _____   yesterday _____

Practice A

And now for the _____ report. Yesterday _____ a cloudy and cool day with a low of 46 degrees. Today _____ partly cloudy and windy with a _____ of rain this evening. The _____ in downtown Boston right _____ is 50. The weather will _____ overnight and tomorrow _____ _____ sunny with a high of 59.

Looking at the _____ weather, Moscow is _____ 5 and cloudy. It's _____ in Paris and the _____ there is 42 degrees. Rio de Janeiro _____ sunny with a temperature of 86. Those people in Rio are very _____ . That's it for today. I'll _____ _____ tomorrow at the same time.

Practice B

1.  +86 F. ★ *What's the weather like today* ?
   ○ *Beautiful. It's sunny and hot* .

2. ![snowman] −5 F. ★ _____ ?
   ○ _____ .

3. ![umbrella] +64 F. ★ _____ ?
   ○ _____ .

4. ![clouds] +92 F. ★ _____ ?
   ○ _____ .

5. ![wind] −10 F. ★ _____ ?
   ○ _____ .

6. ![foggy] +50 F. ★ _____ ?
   ○ _____ .

Practice C

is, was, will be

1. Today *is* _____ Monday.
2. Yesterday _____ Sunday.
3. Tomorrow _____ a hot day.
4. Next month my brother _____ in New York.
5. It _____ warm outside now.
6. It _____ warm yesterday, too.
7. My wife _____ in Washington yesterday.
8. She _____ here tomorrow.
9. My husband _____ at work right now.
10. What _____ the weather like yesterday?

Practice D

1. What's the weather like in your city today?

   _____ .

2. What's the weather like in your city in the winter?

   _____ .

3. What's the weather like in your city in the summer?

   _____ .

4. What was the weather like in your city yesterday?

   _____ .

5. What's the temperature right now?

   _____ .

What time will it leave?

A

○ Thank you for calling Top Airlines. Kathy Smith speaking.
★ What time is the last flight to Toronto tomorrow?
○ The last one is flight number 52 at 8:30 p.m.
★ I'd like to make a reservation for one person, please.
○ Do you want a round trip ticket?
★ Yes.
○ The fare is $249. You have to pick up your ticket thirty minutes before departure.

. . . . (next day). . . . .

★ Is the flight to Toronto on time?
○ No, it's delayed.
★ What time will it leave?
○ At 10:30. You can check your bags now, and go to gate 12.

B

★ Do you have a single room with a bath?
○ Yes, we do. For how many nights?
★ I'm not sure yet. Is it possible to see the room?
○ Certainly. Would you like a room with a balcony?
★ It doesn't matter, but I'd like a quiet room.
○ Fine. Please follow me.

I'd like a double room with a shower.
I'd like a room with an air conditioner.
I'd like a room at the front.

C

○ Metro Taxi.
★ Could you send a taxi to the Rex Hotel, please?
○ Your name, please?
★ Ms. Harris.
○ Thank you.
★ How long will it take?
○ Your taxi will be there in about ten minutes.
★ OK. I'll wait in the lobby.

. . . .

★ How much is the fare to the Royal Museum?
■ It's about $6.00.
★ OK. Could you take me there, please?

Practice A

(i)

○ Thank you for _____ Top Airlines, Kathy Smith _____ .

★ What time is the _____ _____ to Toronto tomorrow?

○ The last one is flight number 52 at 8:30 p.m.

★ I'd like to make a _____ for one _____ , please.

○ Do you want a _____ trip ticket?

★ Yes.

○ The _____ is $249. You have to _____ _____ your ticket thirty minutes before _____ .

Practice B

(i)

★ _____ _____ _____ a single room with a bath?

○ Yes, we do. For _____ _____ nights?

★ I'm not _____ yet. Is it _____ to see the room?

○ Certainly. _____ _____ like a room with a balcony?

★ It doesn't _____ , but I'd like a _____ room.

○ Fine. Please _____ me.

Practice C

(i)

○ Metro Taxi.

★ Could you _____ a taxi to the Rex Hotel, please?

○ Your _____ , please?

★ Ms. Harris.

○ Thank you.

★ How long _____ it _____ ?

○ Your taxi _____ _____ there in about ten minutes.

★ OK. I'll _____ in the lobby.

Dictionary

airline _____   gate _____
check _____   last _____
delayed _____   on time _____
departure _____   person _____
fare _____   reservation _____

(ii)
Write these conversations on a piece of paper.

1. flight / New York / 2:15
   ★ *Is the flight to New York on time?*
   ○ *No, I'm sorry. That flight is delayed.*
   ★ *What time will it leave?*
   ○ *At two fifteen.*
2. bus / Chicago / 9:30
3. train / Washington / 11:45
4. _____ / _____ / _____

Dictionary

air conditioner _____   follow _____
balcony _____   possible _____
certainly _____   single _____
double _____   yet _____

(ii)
Write these conversations on a piece of paper.

1. single / bath / color TV / quiet room
   ★ *Do you have a single room with a bath?*
   ○ *Yes, we do. Would you like a room with a color TV?*
   ★ *It doesn't matter, but I'd like a quiet room.*
2. double / air conditioner / balcony / at the back
3. single / shower / at the front / color TV
4. _____ / _____ / _____ / _____

Dictionary

lobby _____   send _____

(ii)
Write these conversations on a piece of paper.

1. 25 Hill St. / #2701 / 20 minutes
   ★ *Could you send a taxi to 25 Hill Street, please?*
   ○ *Is that an apartment?*
   ★ *Yes, it's apartment number 2701.*
   ★ *How long will it take?*
   ○ *About twenty minutes.*
2. 3507 Lake Rd. / #52 / half an hour
3. 553 Sunset Ave. / No, it's a house / 15 minutes
4. _____ / _____ / _____

Yesterday I went to . . . .

Dear Linda,

I'm on vacation in Toronto. There are a lot of things to do here. Two days ago I went to the top of the CN tower. The view was fantastic! Yesterday I went to the art gallery and tomorrow I'm going to Toronto Island. I met some American tourists this morning, and we had lunch together at a sidewalk café. They were very interesting people. After lunch I went shopping and I bought a dress at a boutique. Prices are low here. I only paid $25. I'm going home in a few days, but I'm having so much fun that I want to stay here. Take care!

Love,
Nancy

CANADA
POSTAGE
POSTES 32

Miss Linda Evans

200 Shaw St.

Boston, MA 02109

U.S.A.

①

②

③

④

⑤

A. ★ When is your vacation?
○ Next month.
★ Are you going to Mexico?
○ No, I'm going to Hawaii.
I went to Mexico last year.
★ I hope you have a nice trip.
○ Thanks.

B. ★ Did you go to Japan last year?
○ No, I didn't.
★ Where did you go?
○ I went to France.
★ Did you have a good time?
○ Yes, I did.

61

👉	two days <u>ago</u>	<u>last</u> night
	six weeks <u>ago</u>	<u>last</u> week
	ten years <u>ago</u>	<u>last</u> year

Dictionary

ago _____   last year _____
fantastic _____   top _____
few _____   trip _____
fun _____   view _____
island _____   were _____

PRESENT—PAST		PAST	
go . . . . . . went	I		Did you go . . . ?
have . . . . had	You		
buy . . . . . . bought	He		Yes, I went . . . .
meet . . . . met	She went		
pay . . . . . paid	It		No, I <u>didn't</u> go . . . .
	We		
	They		did not → didn't

Practice A

_____ Linda,

I'm on _____ in Toronto. _____

_____ a lot of things to do here. Two days

ago I _____ to the top of the CN tower. The

view _____ fantastic! Yesterday I _____

to the art gallery and tomorrow _____

_____ to Toronto Island. I _____ some

American tourists this morning and we

_____ lunch together at a sidewalk cafe.

They _____ very interesting people. After

lunch I went shopping and I _____ a dress

at a boutique. _____ are low here. I only

_____ $25.

_____ _____ home in a few days, but

I'm having so much fun that I want to _____

here. Take care!

                                Love,
                                  Nancy

Practice B

Write these conversations on a piece of paper.

1. next month / Mexico / Hawaii / last year
   ★ *When is your vacation?*
   ○ *Next month.*
   ★ *Are you going to Mexico?*
   ○ *No, I'm going to Hawaii. I went to Mexico last year.*
2. in two weeks / Japan / Hong Kong / 2 years ago
3. next August / France / Germany / last year
4. _____ / _____ / _____ / _____

Practice C

Write these conversations on a piece of paper.

1. Brazil / last year / Japan
   ★ *Did you go to Brazil last year?*
   ○ *No, I didn't.*
   ★ *Where did you go?*
   ○ *I went to Japan.*
2. France / two years ago / Germany
3. a movie / last night / a party
4. _____ / _____ / _____

Practice D

**Use these verbs in the present or past.
be, go, have, meet, buy**

1. I _*bought*_ a new car last week.
2. I _____ dinner with my sister-in-law
   yesterday.
3. She _____ an interesting man at the
   party last night.
4. My parents _____ in New York now.
5. They _____ in Washington three weeks
   ago.
6. Who did she _____ at the party?
7. Where did you _____ your dress?
8. He _____ to the beach an hour ago.

Practice E

Write these conversations on a piece of paper.

1. department store / a radio / $90
   ★ *Where did you go yesterday?*
   ○ *I went to the department store.*
   ★ *What did you buy?*
   ○ *I bought a radio.*
   ★ *How much did you pay?*
   ○ *I paid ninety dollars.*
2. camera store / some color film / $5
3. furniture store / a sofa / $450
4. clothing store / a jacket / $79
5. _____ / _____ / _____

A wonderful trip.

Last year, Jeff and Nora Marshall went to Mexico for two weeks. They started their trip on the Pacific coast because they wanted to relax in the sun. They stayed in a small hotel with a swimming pool. In the evenings they sat by the pool and talked, ate tropical fruit and drank different kinds of fruit juices.

During the second week they rented a car and drove through the desert. Then they visited a town in the mountains. Life was difficult in the town and the people worked very hard, especially the women. Jeff and Nora walked around the town and looked at the old buildings and churches. Before they returned to the

coast, they bought some souvenirs in the market and took some photographs. On the drive back they saw many interesting animals and trees. They were surprised at the size and natural beauty of Mexico. When they left, they felt tired, but happy. Their trip was a wonderful experience.

REGULAR VERBS					IRREGULAR VERBS			
work (present)... worked (past)	looked	started	visited		eat (present)....ate (past)	drink...drank	leave.... left	
verb ....verb + ed	rented	stayed	walked		verb ....past form	drive ...drove	see .....saw	
	returned	talked	wanted			eat ....ate	sit ....sat	
						feel....... felt	take ...took	

Dictionary

animals _____   experience _____   return _____   through _____
coast _____   life _____   souvenirs _____ wonderful _____
desert _____   mountains _____

Practice A

Last year, Jeff and Nora Marshall _____ to Mexico for two weeks. They _____ their trip on the Pacific coast because they _____ to relax in the sun. They _____ in a small hotel with a swimming pool. In the evenings they _____ by the pool and talked, _____ tropical fruit and _____ different kinds of fruit juices.

During the second week they _____ a car and _____ through the desert. Then they _____ a town in the mountains. Life _____ difficult in the town and the people _____ very hard, especially the women. Jeff and Nora _____ around the town and _____ at the old buildings and churches. Before they _____ to the coast, they _____ some souvenirs in the market and _____ some photographs. On the drive back they _____ many interesting animals and trees. They _____ surprised at the size and natural beauty of Mexico. When they _____ , they _____ tired, but happy. Their trip _____ a wonderful experience.

Practice B

1. How long did Jeff and Nora stay in Mexico?
   _____
2. Where did they start their trip?
   _____
3. Why did they start there?
   _____
4. Where did they stay?
   _____
5. What did they do in the evenings?
   _____
6. Where did they go during the second week?
   _____
7. Did they drive or did they take a bus?
   _____
8. What did they do in the town?
   _____
9. Where did they buy souvenirs?
   _____
10. What did they see on the drive back?
    _____
11. How did they feel when they left Mexico?
    _____
12. Did they have a good time?
    _____

Practice C

Write these conversations on a piece of paper.

1. go to Hawaii / Mexico
   ★ *Did you go to Hawaii?*
   ○ *No, I didn't. I went to Mexico.*
2. start on the Atlantic coast / Pacific coast
3. stay in a big hotel / small hotel
4. eat American food / Mexican food
5. rent a motorcycle / car
6. drive to Mexico City / a town in the mountains
7. buy souvenirs in your hotel / the market
8. take photos of the people / the buildings
9. see many tourists / only Mexicans
10. feel unhappy about your trip / happy

Where were you?

A

★ Where were you last week?
○ I was in New York.
★ How long were you there?
○ For three days.
★ Was your wife with you?
○ No, she wasn't. She had to work.

B

★ Did you buy any souvenirs in Mexico?
○ Yes, I bought a few things.
★ What did you buy for your brother?
○ I bought him a leather belt.
★ Did you get anything for your parents?
○ Yes, I got them a book about Mexico.

C

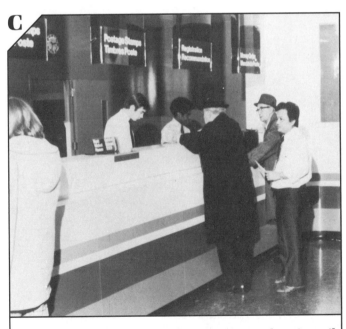

★ I want to send this package to Japan by airmail.
○ That's $2.75.
★ I also need five 10¢ stamps.
○ Did you say ten 5¢ stamps?
★ No, I said five 10¢ stamps.

D

★ I'd like to cash a traveler's check, please.
○ Do you have any identification?
★ Yes, here is my passport.
○ That's fine, and could you sign here, please?
★ Yes. By the way, is the bank open on Saturdays?
○ No, it's closed. We're open from ten to three, Monday to Friday.

65

Was he		No, he wasn't.	PRESENT—PAST	
Was she		No, she wasn't.	get	.... got
Were you	in New York last week?	No, I wasn't.	give	.... gave
Were they		No, they weren't.	have to	.... had to
			say	.... said
			send	.... sent

Dictionary

air mail _____   passport _____
cash _____   traveler's check _____
package _____

Practice A

A. ★ Where _____ _____ last week?

   ○ I _____ in New York.

   ★ How long _____ _____ there?

   ○ _____ three days.

   ★ _____ your wife with you?

   ○ No, she _____ . She had to work.

B. ★ Did you _____ any souvenirs in Mexico?

   ○ Yes, I _____ a few things.

   ★ What _____ _____ buy _____
   your brother?

   ○ I bought _____ a leather belt.

   ★ Did you _____ anything _____
   your parents?

   ○ Yes, I _____ _____ a book about
   Mexico.

Practice D

★ What did you give *to* <u>your wife</u>?	★ What did you buy *for* <u>your parents</u>?
○ I gave <u>her</u> a new dress.	○ I bought <u>them</u> some flowers.
★ What did you send *to* <u>your friends</u>?	★ What did you get *for* <u>your son</u>?
○ I sent <u>them</u> some photos.	○ I got <u>him</u> a book.

give send } something *to* 👤	buy get } something *for* 👤

1. buy / your mother / a book
What did you buy for your mother _____ ?
I bought her a book _____ .

2. give / your husband / a new shirt
_____ ?
_____ .

Practice B

Write these conversations on a piece of paper.

1. last week / Boston / two days / wife / at work
★ *Where were you last week?* _____
○ *I was in Boston.* _____
★ *How long were you there?* _____
○ *For two days.* _____
★ *Was your wife with you?* _____
○ *No, she wasn't. She was at work.* _____

2. last week / Miami / a week / mother / Dallas

3. last night / a party / two hours / husband / at home

4. yesterday / the beach / a few hours / children / at school

5. _____ / _____ / _____ / _____ / _____

Practice C

★ Where were you born?
○ I was born in Japan.

1. Where were you born? _____

2. When were you born? _____

3. Where were you last night? _____

4. Were you in the U.S.A. ten years ago? _____

3. send / your grandparents / a postcard
_____ ?
_____ .

4. get / your daughter / a bicycle
_____ ?
_____ .

5. send / Mr. Badali / an application form
_____ ?
_____ .

6. buy / your aunt / a new blouse
_____ ?
_____ .

7. give / the children / some money
_____ ?
_____ .

What are you going to do?

★ When is your vacation, Mary?

○ Next month. I'm going to visit my sister in California. What are your plans, Nora?

★ Jeff and I are going to Haiti.

○ Haiti! What are you going to do there?

★ Well, I'm going to lie on a nice quiet beach and do nothing. I really need a rest.

○ What's Jeff going to do?

★ He's going to take photos of the people and the old architecture.

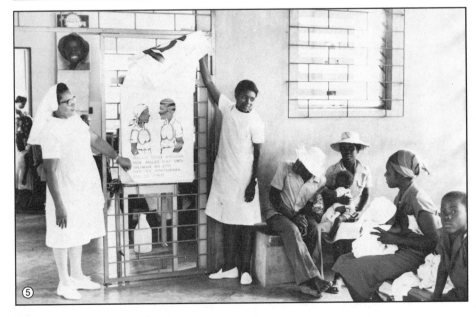

○ Don't you have a friend in Haiti?

★ Yes. He works in a health clinic. We're going to rent a jeep and visit him.

○ Why are you going to rent a jeep?

★ Because the clinic is in the mountains and our friend says the roads are in bad condition.

○ It sounds like you're going to have an exciting trip.

★ I think so, too. I'll send you a postcard.

FUTURE PLAN:
$\begin{cases} \text{I} & \text{am} \\ \text{He/She/It} & \text{is} \\ \text{You/We/They} & \text{are} \end{cases}$ + going to [verb] .   I'm going to go to Haiti. = I'm going to Haiti.

Dictionary

architecture _____   condition _____   lie _____   postcard _____
clinic _____   exciting _____   plan _____   rest _____

Practice A

★ When is your vacation, Mary?

○ Next month. I'm going _____ _____
my sister in California. What are your _____ ,
Nora?

★ Jeff and I _____ _____ to Haiti.

○ Haiti! What are you going _____
_____ there?

★ Well, I'm _____ _____ lie on a nice quiet
beach and do _____ . I really need a rest.

○ _____ Jeff going to do?

★ He's going _____ _____ photos of
the people and the old architecture.

○ Don't you _____ a friend in Haiti?

★ Yes. He _____ in a health clinic.
_____ _____ to rent a jeep and visit him.

○ Why _____ _____ going to rent a jeep?

★ Because the clinic is in the mountains and our
friend _____ the roads are in bad condition.

○ It sounds like you're going _____
_____ an exciting trip.

★ I think so, too. I'll _____ you a postcard.

Practice B

1. What are Mary's plans?
_____

2. What's Nora going to do in Haiti?
_____

3. What's Jeff going to do?
_____

4. Who are Jeff and Nora going to visit?
_____

5. Where does their friend work?
_____

6. How are they going to get there?
_____

7. Why do they need a jeep?
_____

Practice C

1. What are you going to do tonight?
_____

2. What time are you going to go to bed?
_____

3. What time are you going to get up tomorrow?
_____

4. Where are you going to go tomorrow?
_____

Practice D

1. the teacher / start the class
   When is the teacher going to start the class ?
2. Maria / make dinner
   When _____ ?
3. you / visit me
   When _____ ?
4. Tom / fix his car
   When _____ ?
5. they / sell their house
   When _____ ?
6. we /go dancing
   When _____ ?

Practice E

1. I/visit   *I'm going to visit* my sister next month.
2. I/visit   *I visited* my brother last month.
3. We/drive   _____ to Toronto yesterday.
4. They/see   _____ a good movie last night.
5. She/take   _____ a taxi to work tomorrow.
6. She/take Yesterday, _____ the subway.
7. We/see   _____ a movie tomorrow night.
8. He/rent   _____ a new car next month.
9. I/leave   _____ Chile in June, 1983.
10. They/eat   _____ dinner in two hours.

REVIEW/Lessons 25—30

WHICH ONE IS IT?

1. a. I have to work.
   b. I had to work.

2. a. They were at home.
   b. They weren't at home.

3. a. They aren't happy.
   b. They weren't happy.

4. a. They start at 8 o'clock.
   b. They started at 8 o'clock.

5. a. We stay in a hotel.
   b. We stayed in a hotel.

6. a. I work until 9:30.
   b. I worked until 9:30.

7. a. Where do you go?
   b. Where did you go?

8. a. Did she have a good time?
   b. Did you have a good time?

9. a. What are you going to do?
   b. What are they going to do?

YES OR NO?

1. Yesterday was a cool day.   YES   NO

2. Yesterday was sunny.   YES   NO

3. Today it's windy.   YES   NO

4. Maybe it will rain this evening.   YES   NO

5. It's cold in Dallas right now.   YES   NO

6. The high tomorrow will be 76.   YES   NO

7. The weather in London is nice.   YES   NO

8. It's raining in Tokyo.   YES   NO

9. There will be a weather report tomorrow.   YES   NO

FINISH THE CONVERSATIONS WITH THE CORRECT FORM OF: is, are, do, does, did.

1. ★ _Do_ you go to school every morning?
   ○ No, I _don't_ go to school every morning.

2. ★ _____ you go downtown last night?
   ○ No, I _____ go downtown last night.

3. ★ _____ your sister visit you yesterday?
   ○ No, she _____ visit me yesterday.

4. ★ _____ your sister usually visit you?
   ○ No, she _____ usually visit me.

5. ★ _____ Jeff going to drive to New York.
   ○ No, he _____ going to drive to New York.

6. ★ _____ your friends going to stay in a hotel?
   ○ No, they _____ going to stay in a hotel.

7. ★ _____ he leave two days ago?
   ○ No, he _____ leave two days ago.

8. ★ _____ the train leave at 9:30 every evening?
   ○ No, it _____ leave at 9:30 every evening.

9. ★ _____ she going to buy a new car?
   ○ No, she _____ going to buy a new car.

10. ★ _____ you think English is easy?
    ○ No, I _____ think English is easy.

DISCOVER/Lessons 25–30
Discover A

1. give/gave

2. wear/wore

3. make/made

4. speak/spoke

5. come/came

6. do/did

7. forget/forgot

8. write/wrote

9. live/lived [d]

10. study/studied [d]

11. finish/finished [t]

12. wait/waited [id]

1. ★ _Did you give_ her some chocolates?
   ○ _No, I didn't. I gave her some flowers._

2. ★ _____ blue jeans to the party?
   ○ _____

3. ★ _____ chicken for dinner?
   ○ _____

4. ★ _____ Spanish to the teacher?
   ○ _____

5. ★ _____ to New York by bus?
   ○ _____

6. ★ _____ your English lessons last night?
   ○ _____

7. ★ _____ your purse?
   ○ _____

8. ★ _____ to your parents?
   ○ _____

9. ★ _____ in an apartment in Boston?
   ○ _____

10. ★ _____ economics at the university?
    ○ _____

11. ★ _____ work at 5:00?
    ○ _____

12. ★ _____ in front of the movie theater?
    ○ _____

Discover B

Use the present or past form of these verbs in the conversations.
  be, do, forget, have to, live, stay, study, wait

1. ★ How long did you _live_ in Japan?
   ○ I _____ there for two years.

2. ★ What did you _____ on the weekend?
   ○ I _____ home and _____ English.

3. ★ How long did you _____ for the bus?
   ○ Not long. I _____ for about five minutes.

4. ★ Why _____ you late last night?
   ○ Because I _____ my bus tickets so I _____ walk.

70

How much will it cost?

1. Fill it up and check the oil, please.

2.

3.

4. That's $12.50 total.

Here you go.

Thanks.

5. How's the car running?

Not bad, but the brakes aren't working very well. I'm going to check them at home.

I'll check them for you. Bring your car inside. I'll give you a free estimate.

PETRO-DOLLARS REDEEMED HERE!

GULF MEANS MORE

6.

7. The brakes are in poor condition. They need a lot of work.

How much will it cost?

With parts and labor, it'll be about $200.

8. $200! I can't afford that!

I'm sorry, but I can't do it for less.

OK. I'll think about it and let you know tomorrow.

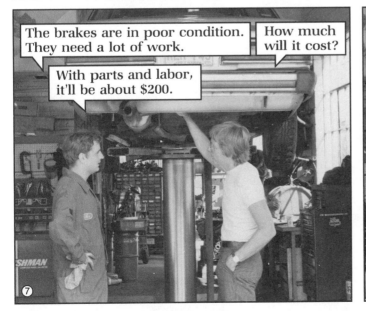

☞ I'm going to check the brakes. (PLAN, INTENT)
I'll check the brakes for you. (OFFER)

Dictionary

afford _____ free _____
brakes _____ inside _____
bring _____ labor _____
cost _____ less _____
estimate _____ parts _____

Practice A

★ _____ it up and _____ the oil, please.

○ That's $12.50 total.

★ Here you go.

○ Thanks. _____ the car running?

★ Not bad, but the brakes aren't _____ very well. _____ _____ to check them at home.

○ _____ check them for you. _____ your car inside. _____ give you a free estimate.

· · · · · · · · · ·

○ The brakes are in poor _____ . They need _____ _____ _____ work.

★ How much _____ _____ cost?

○ With parts and labor, it'll _____ about $200.

★ $200! I _____ _____ that!

○ I'm sorry, but I _____ _____ it for less.

★ OK. I'll _____ it and let you _____ tomorrow.

Practice C

Write these conversations on a piece of paper.

1. TV /$75
   ★ *My TV isn't working.*
   ○ *OK. I'll check it for you.*
   ★ *How much will it cost?*
   ○ *Seventy-five dollars.*
   ★ *I can't afford that.*
   ○ *Sorry, I can't do it for less.*
   ★ *OK. I'll think about it and let you know tomorrow.*
2. refrigerator / $55
3. brakes / $230
4. watch / $40
5. _____ / _____

Practice B

1. open the window
   ★ *I'm going to open the window.*
   ○ *Sit down. I'll open it for you.*
   ★ *Oh, thank you.*

2. type this letter
   ★ _____
   ○ _____
   ★ _____

3. wash the dishes
   ★ _____
   ○ _____
   ★ _____

4. get the newspaper
   ★ _____
   ○ _____
   ★ _____

5. call the children
   ★ _____
   ○ _____
   ★ _____

6. make dinner
   ★ _____
   ○ _____
   ★ _____

Practice D

1. **bring, come, have**
   ★ Hello, Jamie. I'm going to _____ a party on Friday night. Would you like to _____ ?
   ○ Sure! I'll _____ my new cassette player.

2. **bring, do, fix, need**
   ★ What are you going to _____ on the weekend?
   ○ I'm going to _____ my car.
   ★ Do you _____ any help?
   ○ Sure. Thanks!
   ★ Good. I'll _____ my tools.

3. **know, need, take, visit**
   ★ Are you and Bill going to _____ your parents on Sunday?
   ○ I don't _____ yet. We _____ someone to _____ care of the children.
   ★ I'll do it for you.
   ○ Oh, thanks! That's very nice of you.

How does it look?

At the restaurant

★ What are you going to have?

○ I'm going to order a tuna sandwich. What about you?

★ I'm not sure. I think I'll have a small salad.

At work

★ What are you going to do after work?

○ I'm going to visit my sister. What about you?

★ I don't know yet. Maybe I'll go home and watch TV.

73

☞ I'm going to have a salad. (CERTAIN)
   Maybe I'll have a salad. (UNCERTAIN)

Try on the jacket. = Try it on.

Dictionary _____

agree _____   positive _____
charge _____   reasonable _____
label _____   try on _____
percent _____   upstairs _____

Practice A _____

★ That's a nice sports jacket.

○ I _____ .

★ I think _____ go inside.

★ Excuse me. Where _____ the men's sports
jackets?

■ _____ at the front of the store.

★ Here's the jacket we _____ in the window.

○ You _____ check the price first.

★ It only _____ $89. That's very reasonable.

○ _____ at the _____ and check the
size and the material.

★ It's my _____ and it's one hundred

percent wool. _____ _____

_____ try it on.

★ It feels OK. How _____ _____ look?

○ It _____ great!

★ Are you _____ ?

○ I'm _____ .

★ Then, _____ _____ _____ buy it.

■ _____ that be cash or charge?

★ Cash.

At the restaurant

★ What are you _____ _____ have?

○ I'm _____ _____ order a tuna
sandwich. What about you?

★ I'm not sure. I think _____ have a small
salad.

At work

★ What are you going to _____ after work?

○ I'm going to visit my sister. What about you?

★ I don't _____ yet. Maybe _____

_____ home and watch TV.

Practice B _____

Answer these questions about the photo story.

1. Last Saturday John and his friend went
shopping. What did John see in the store
window?

_____

2. Where were the men's sports jackets?

_____

3. How much did the jacket cost?

_____

4. Why did he look at the label?

_____

5. What kind of material was the jacket?

_____

6. How did the jacket look?

_____

7. Did John buy it?

_____

8. How did he pay for the jacket, by cash or by
charge?

_____

Practice C _____

Write these conversations on a piece of paper.

1. order a sandwich / have a salad
   ★ *I'm going to order a steak. What about you?*
   ○ *I think I'll have a salad.*
2. order some soup / have a hamburger
3. watch TV / study English
4. clean the house / go to bed
5. _____ / _____

Practice D _____

★ This TV program is terrible.
○ Then turn it off.

Turn off the TV. → Turn it off.
Take off your shoes. → Take them off.

1. Turn off the TV.   *Turn it off.*
2. Try on this jacket. _____
3. Try on these shoes. _____
4. Turn on the radio.   _____
5. Take off your gloves. _____
6. Put on your sweater. _____
7. Pick up the books.   _____

What size do you wear?

A

★ salesperson   ○ customer

★ May I help you?
○ No, thanks. I'm just looking
★ OK. Let me know if you need any help.
. . . .

○ Excuse me. Could I try on these pants?
★ Sure, the fitting room is over there.
. . . .

★ How are they?
○ They're too short. Do you have a bigger size?
★ Yes, we do.
. . . .

★ Do they fit?
○ Yes, but do you think they look all right?
★ They look very nice on you.
○ OK, I'll take them.

B

★ salesperson   ○ customer

○ I'd like to try on these shoes.
★ What size do you wear?
○ I'm not sure. I think size seven.
. . . .

★ How are they?
○ They're too big. Do you have a smaller size?
★ Yes, we do. Here you are.
. . . .

○ These are perfect. How much are they?
★ $200. Do you want them?
○ No, thanks. I'd like to think about it first.

☞ ◯ ◯ ◯ ◯
big bigger small smaller

Dictionary

all right _____   fitting room _____   loose _____   short _____
fit _____   long _____   perfect _____   tight _____

Practice A

A. ★ _____ I help you?

○ No, thanks. I'm _____ _____ .

★ OK. _____ me _____ if you need any help.

· · · · · · · · · · ·

○ Excuse me. Could I _____ _____ these pants?

★ Sure, the _____ room is over there.

· · · · · · · · · · ·

★ How are they?

○ They're _____ short. Do you have a _____ size?

★ Yes, we do.

· · · · · · · · · · ·

★ Do they _____ ?

○ Yes, but do you _____ they look all right?

★ They look very nice on you.

○ OK, I'll _____ _____ .

B. ○ I'd like _____ _____ _____ these shoes.

★ What size _____ _____ _____ ?

○ I'm _____ sure. I _____ size seven.

· · · · · · · · · · · · ·

★ How are they?

○ They're _____ big. Do you have a _____ size?

★ Yes, we do. Here you are.

· · · · · · · · · · ·

○ _____ are perfect. How much _____ they?

★ $200. Do you _____ _____ ?

○ No, thanks. I'd like to think _____ _____ first.

Practice B

1. _Where is the fitting room_ _____ ?
   The fitting room is at the back of the store.

2. _____ ?
   The children's clothes are on the third floor.

3. _____ ?
   I wear size seven and a half.

4. _____ ?
   It looks great!

5. _____ ?
   I bought my dress at Gigi's boutique.

6. _____ ?
   Yes, this store is open on Saturdays.

7. _____ ?
   Yes, I went shopping on the weekend.

8. _____ ?
   Yes, I'm going to buy it.

9. _____ ?
   Yes, it's one hundred percent cotton.

10. _____ ?
   No, we don't have that dress in a different color.

Practice C

Write these conversations on a piece of paper.

1. shoes / tight
   ★ _How do those shoes fit?_
   ○ _They're too tight. Do you have a bigger size?_
   ★ _Yes, I'll get them for you._

2. pants / long

3. hat / small

4. gloves / big

5. skirt / loose

6. belt / tight

7. _____ / _____

Can you lend me . . . ?

A

★ Susan, I don't know which record to buy.

○ I like this one by Bravo better.

★ The other one is cheaper.

○ Yes, but it isn't as good as the Bravo record.

★ You're right, but I don't have enough money. Can you lend me five dollars?

○ When can you pay me back?

★ Next Friday.

○ OK.

        . . . (next Friday). . . . .

○ Lisa, did you bring the money?

★ Sorry, I forgot. I'll bring it tomorrow.

B

★ How much is this TV?

○ It's five hundred dollars. And that one is four hundred dollars.

★ Why is this one more expensive?

○ Because it's better quality.

_____

★ How much is this radio?

○ It's seventy dollars. And that one is ninety.

★ Why is this one less expensive?

○ Because it's on sale.

C

★ I want to return these pants.

○ What's wrong with them?

★ The zipper is broken.

○ Do you have the sales slip?

★ Yes, I do.

○ Would you like an exchange or a refund?

★ A refund, please.

_____

★ What's wrong with this shirt?

○ It's the wrong size and a button is missing.

☞ less expensive = cheaper

as <u>good</u> as

as ⬚adjective⬚ as

Dictionary

broken _____   lend _____   quality _____   sales slip _____
button _____   missing _____   record _____   wrong _____
exchange _____   on sale _____   refund _____   zipper _____

Practice A

(i)

★ Susan, I don't know _____ record to buy.

○ I like this one by Bravo _____ .

★ The other one is _____ .

○ Yes, but it isn't _____ good _____ the Bravo record.

★ You're right, but I don't have _____ money. Can you _____ _____ five dollars?

○ When can you _____ _____ back?

★ Next Friday.

○ OK.

(ii)

Write these conversations on a piece of paper.

1. $10 / record / tomorrow
   ★ *Can you lend me ten dollars?*
   ○ *What for?*   (What for? = Why?)
   ★ *I want to buy a record.*
   ○ *When can you pay me back?*
   ★ *Tomorrow.*
   ○ *OK.*

2. a dollar / bus ticket / tomorrow morning
3. $20 / a shirt / next Thursday
4. $1,000 / a car / in six months
5. _____ / _____ / _____

Practice B

(i)

★ How much _____ this TV?

○ _____ five hundred dollars. And that one is four hundred dollars.

★ Why is this one _____ expensive?

○ Because it's _____ quality.

· · · · · · · · · · · · · ·

★ How much _____ this radio?

○ _____ seventy dollars. And that one is ninety.

★ Why is this one _____ expensive?

○ Because it's _____ _____ .

(ii)

Write these conversations on a piece of paper.

1. jacket / $80 / $100
   ★ *How much is this jacket?*
   ○ *It's eighty dollars, and that one is a hundred dollars.*
   ★ *Why is this one less expensive?*
   ○ *Because it's on sale.*

2. sofa / $400 / $600
3. carpet / $2,000 / $1,800
4. cassette player / $120 / $95
5. _____ / _____ / _____

Practice C

(i)

★ I want _____ _____ these pants.

○ What's _____ with them?

★ The zipper is _____ .

○ _____ _____ have the sales slip?

★ Yes, I do.

○ _____ _____ like an exchange or a refund?

★ A refund, please.

(ii)

Write these conversations on a piece of paper.

1. watch / doesn't work
   ★ *I'd like to return this watch.*
   ○ *What's wrong with it?*
   ★ *It doesn't work.*
   ○ *Would you like an exchange or a refund?*
   ★ *An exchange, please.*

2. blouse / two buttons are missing
3. dress / my wife doesn't like the color
4. _____ / _____

At the supermarket.

A

★ Hi, Don. I didn't know you shopped at this supermarket.

○ Yes, I shop here once a week.

★ Wow! You sure buy a lot of things. Bread, milk, butter, cigarettes. . . . I didn't know you smoked. How many cigarettes do you smoke a day?

○ About a pack a day.

★ That's a lot! I don't smoke because it's bad for my health. Oh, you have coffee, too. How much coffee do you drink?

○ Five or six cups a day.

★ That's a lot! I don't drink much coffee because it makes me nervous. Oh, by the way, where is the ice cream?

○ It's in the frozen food section. That's aisle three, on the right.

★ Thanks. See you later.

B

> 👉 How <u>much</u> coffee do you drink? I drink a lot of coffee. I smoke a lot of cigarettes.
> How <u>many</u> cigarette<u>s</u> do you smoke? I do<u>n't</u> drink <u>much</u> coffee. I do<u>n't</u> smoke <u>many</u> cigarettes.

Dictionary

aisle _____ dairy _____ frozen _____ section _____
beverage _____ flour _____ meat _____ steak _____
canned _____ fresh _____ nervous _____

Practice A

★ Hi, Don. I ____ ____ you shopped at this supermarket.

○ Yes, I shop here ____ a week.

★ Wow! You sure buy ____ ____ ____ things. Bread, milk, butter, cigarettes . . . I didn't know you smoked. ____ ____ cigarettes do you smoke a day?

○ About a pack a day.

★ That's ____ ____ ! I don't smoke because it's bad for my health. Oh, you have

coffee, too. ____ ____ coffee do you drink?

○ Five or six cups a day.

★ That's ____ ____ ! I ____ drink ____ coffee because it makes me nervous. Oh, by the way, where ____ the ice cream?

○ It's in the ____ food section. That's ____ three, on the right.

★ Thanks. See you later.

Practice B

Look at the picture of the supermarket on page 79, and write these conversations.

1. canned tomatoes
   ★ *Where are the canned tomatoes* ?
   ○ *They're in the canned food section, aisle two on the left* .
2. flour
   ★ ____ ?
   ○ ____ .
3. carrots
   ★ ____ ?
   ○ ____ .
4. cheese
   ★ ____ ?
   ○ ____ .
5. steak
   ★ ____ ?
   ○ ____ .
6. frozen dinners
   ★ ____ ?
   ○ ____ .
7. apple juice
   ★ ____ ?
   ○ ____ .

Practice C

many, much

1. cheese / eat *How much cheese do you eat* ?
2. tea / drink ____ ?
3. apples / have ____ ?
4. sugar / want ____ ?
5. money / make ____ ?
6. eggs / use ____ ?
7. stamps / need ____ ?
8. time / have ____ ?

Practice D

many, much

1. eat / vegetables / eggs
   I eat a lot of vegetables, but I don't eat many eggs.
2. drink / milk / coffee
   ____
3. buy / carrots / tomatoes
   ____
4. eat / fish / meat
   ____
5. read / books / magazines
   ____

80

Sorry, we don't have any . . . .

A

★ Would you like to order now?

○ Yes, I'd like some tomato soup, please.

★ I'm sorry, we don't have any soup today.

○ Well, then I'd like some French fries.

★ Sorry, we don't have any French fries either. Our cook is sick, so we're out of almost everything.

○ Do you have any milk?

★ Yes, we do.

○ OK, I'll have a glass of milk.

B

★ Would you like some orange juice?

○ No, thanks. I don't want anything to drink right now.

★ How about something to eat?

○ OK. I'll have an apple.

★ Who did you visit on the weekend?

○ Nobody. (I didn't visit anybody.)

★ Where did you go?

○ Nowhere. (I didn't go anywhere.)

★ Well, what did you do?

○ Nothing. (I didn't do anything.)

★ Sounds like you didn't have a good weekend.

C

★ Excuse me. I don't know how to use this machine. Could you show me?

○ Sure. First, put your money in here. Then, select what you want.

★ Now what do I have to do?

○ Just press the button and then take out your coffee.

★ Oh, that was easy. Thanks for your help.

○ You're welcome.

Could you show me how to use this machine?

Could you teach me how to speak English?

Could you tell me how to get to the post office?

I have <u>some</u> milk.   I <u>don't</u> have <u>any</u> milk.
I need <u>some</u> stamps.   I <u>don't</u> need <u>any</u> stamps.
I want <u>something</u> to eat.   I <u>don't</u> want <u>anything</u> to eat.
some .... any (NEGATIVE)

Practice A

A. ★ Would you like _____ _____ now?

○ Yes, I'd like _____ tomato soup, please.

★ I'm sorry, we _____ have _____ soup today.

○ Well, then I'd like _____ French fries.

★ Sorry, we _____ have _____ French fries either. Our cook is sick, so we're out of almost _____ .

○ _____ _____ have any milk?

★ Yes, we do.

○ OK, _____ have a glass of milk.

B. ★ _____ like some orange juice?

○ No, thanks. I _____ want _____ to drink right now.

★ How about _____ to eat?

○ OK. _____ have an apple.

. . . .

★ Who did you visit on the weekend?

○ _____ .

★ Where did you go?

○ _____ .

★ What did you do?

○ _____ .

★ Sounds like you _____ have a good weekend.

C. ★ Excuse me. I don't know _____ to use this machine. Could you _____ _____ ?

○ Sure. First, _____ your money in here. Then, _____ what you want.

★ Now what do I _____ _____ do?

○ Just _____ the button and then _____ _____ your coffee.

★ Oh, that was _____ . Thanks for your _____ .

○ You're _____ .

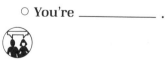

Dictionary

everything _____   select _____
press _____   show _____

Practice B

1. I want some ice cream.
   I don't want any ice cream.

2. I need some money.
   _____

3. I want something to drink.
   _____

4. I have some photos of my family.
   _____

5. I ate some chocolate cake.
   I didn't eat any chocolate cake.

6. I sent some flowers to my mother.
   _____

7. I bought something for my wife.
   _____

8. I had some problems.
   _____

Practice C

a, an, any, anything, some, something

1. No, thanks, I don't want _____ bread.
2. I need _____ batteries for this radio.
3. No, thanks. I don't want _____ to drink.
4. I didn't buy _____ flour, but I bought _____ rice.
5. There is _____ milk in the refrigerator.
6. I didn't tell her _____ .
7. There aren't _____ spoons in the tray.
8. I took _____ photos in Haiti, but I didn't take _____ photos in Mexico.
9. I'll give you _____ to eat, but I'd won't give you _____ money.
10. I don't want _____ to eat, but I'd like _____ cup of tea.
11. I don't need _____ envelope, but I need some stamps.

REVIEW/Lessons 31–36

WHICH ONE IS IT?

1. a. Do you need any help?
   b. Did you need any help?

2. a. They are too big.
   b. They were too big.

3. a. It isn't my size.
   b. It wasn't my size.

4. a. They aren't on sale.
   b. They weren't on sale.

5. a. How much coffee do you drink?
   b. How much coffee did you drink?

6. a. How many eggs does she eat?
   b. How many eggs did she eat?

7. a I'm going to try it on.
   b. I'm going to try them on.

8. a. I can afford that.
   b. I can't afford that.

9. a. I'll do it for you.
   b. We'll do it for you.

WHAT NUMBER IS IT?

FINISH THESE CONVERSATIONS.

1. ★ Can you check my TV? It _isn't_ working.
   ○ OK.
   ★ How _____ will it cost?
   ○ It's _____ bad condition. It'll be about $120 total.
   ★ I _____ afford that!
   ○ I'm _____ , but I can't do _____ for less.
   ★ OK. I'll think _____ it.

2. ★ Can you lend _____ $20?
   ○ What for?
   ★ I want _____ buy this shirt.
   ○ When can you pay me _____ ?
   ★ Next Friday.
   ○ OK, but _____ forget.
   ○ Don't worry. I _____ forget.

DISCOVER/Lessons 31–36
Discover A

a flat tire

an oil leak

a broken headlight

the engine overheats

Use these words to complete the conversations.
engine, headlight, flat, oil leak, need, afford, have, fix, it, one

1. ★ What's wrong with your car?
   ○ The _____ overheats. Can you
   _____ it?
   ★ Sorry, not today.
   ○ When can you do _____ ?
   ★ Tomorrow morning.

2. ★ Hey, Pat! Your car has a _____ tire.
   ○ Which _____ ?
   ★ The back one on the driver's side.

3. ★ Can I _____ three cans of motor oil, please?
   ○ Three cans! That's a lot!
   ★ I know, but there's an _____ in the engine and I can't _____ to fix it.

4. ★ The left _____ on my car is broken. I think I _____ a new one.
   ○ OK. I'll take a look at it right away.

Discover B

a can of tuna

a jar of jam

a box of cookies

a bag of rice

a bottle of soda

a loaf of bread

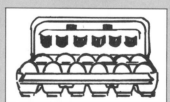

a carton of eggs

a bar of soap

★ I'm going to the supermarket. Do you need anything?

1. ○ Yes. Get me a _carton_ of eggs.
2. ○ Yes. Get me a _____ of honey.
3. ○ Yes. Get me a _____ of soup.
4. ○ Yes. Get me a _____ of soap.
5. ○ Yes. Get me a _____ of detergent.
6. ○ Yes. Get me a _____ of bread.
7. ○ Yes. Get me a _____ of soda.
8. ○ Yes. Get me a _____ of rice.

9. What things do you buy in a can?
   _____ _____ _____
10. What things do you buy in a jar?
   _____ _____ _____
11. What things do you buy in a bottle?
   _____ _____ _____
12. What things do you buy by the pound?
   _____ _____ _____

84

WORD LIST

ANSWER KEY

Lesson 1, page 2
Practice B
2. Is your brother from Tokyo?
   No, he's from Osaka.
3. Is your girl friend from Mexico City?
   No, she's from Acapulco.
4. Are you from New York?
   No, I'm from _____ .
5. Are most of your friends from Boston?
   No, they're from _____ .
6. Is your teacher from Miami?
   No, she's from _____ .
7. Are your parents from Chicago?
   No, they're from _____ .

Practice C
2. ★ Is your sister in Hong Kong?
   ○ No, she isn't.
   ★ Oh, where is she?
   ○ She's in New York.
3. ★ Are your parents in Brazil?
   ○ No, they aren't.
   ★ Oh, where are they?
   ○ They're in Argentina.
4. ★ Is your boyfriend in England?
   ○ No, he isn't.
   ★ Oh, where is he?
   ○ He's in France.

Lesson 2, page 4
Practice B
2. ★ What do you do?
   ○ I'm a mechanic.
   ★ Where do you work?
   ○ In a garage on Bedford Rd.
3. ★ What do you do?
   ○ I'm a waitress.
   ★ Where do you work?
   ○ In a restaurant on Lakeshore Ave.
4. ★ What do you do?
   ○ I'm a cashier.
   ★ Where do you work?
   ○ In a hardware store on Front St.

Practice C
2. ★ Do you live in an apartment?
   ○ Yes, I have a big apartment on the fifth floor.
   ★ Do you live alone?
   ○ No, I live with my family.
3. ★ Do you live in an apartment?
   ○ Yes I have a small apartment on the third floor.
   ★ Do you live alone?
   ○ No, I live with my husband and daughter.
4. ★ Do you live in an apartment?
   ○ Yes, I have a nice apartment on the second floor.

★ Do you live alone?
○ No, I live with my sister.

Lesson 3, page 6
Practice B
2. Are you . . . I am   5. Are you, I'm not
3. Do you, I do   6. Are you, I am
4. Do you, I don't   7. Do you, I do

Practice C
2. Where do you live?
3. Who do you live with?
4. Where are you from?
5. What city do you live in?
6. What do you study?
7. How are you?

Practice E
2. in   4. on   6. at
3. at   5. on   7. in

Listening Activity
A. 1. seat   6. this
   2. sit   7. sixth
   3. eat   8. miss
   4. it   9. meet
   5. these   10. office
B. 1. a 2. b 3. a 4. a 5. a

Lesson 4, page 8
Practice B
1. She likes vanilla ice cream.
2. He likes chocolate ice cream.
3. He likes to drink coffee.
4. His wife prefers tea.
5. She likes to read books in her spare time.
6. He has a bicycle.
7. Yes, they are happy.

Practice D
2. need   8. buy   14. studies
3. goes   9. works   15. get up
4. like   10. pay   16. eats
5. has   11. lives   17. know
6. drives   12. speak
7. drink   13. come

Lesson 5, page 10
Practice B
2. Does your wife have a new job?
3. Do you usually come here?
4. Does Kim study economics?
5. Do you miss your family and friends?
6. Do your friends live in New York?
7. Does your brother like to read?
8. Does that machine work?
9. Does your daughter need some medicine?
10. Do your parents speak English?

Practice C
1. doesn't   6. aren't
2. don't, aren't   7. doesn't
3. isn't, doesn't   8. don't, isn't
4. don't   9. Don't, doesn't
5. isn't   10. doesn't

Lesson 6, page 12
Practice B
2. ★ How do I get to City Hall?
   ○ Take the King subway line north. Get off at Front St. Then transfer to the number 15 bus east.
3. ★ How do I get to Central Hospital?
   ○ Take the number 6 bus west. Get off at Fifth St. Then walk two blocks north.
4. ★ How do I get to the post office?
   ○ Take the number 13 bus north. Transfer to the University subway line east. Get off at Eighth St.
5. ★ How do I get to the Ritz Hotel?
   ○ Take the Main subway line south. Get off at Lakeshore Avenue. Then walk one block west.

Practice C
2. ★ Excuse me. Is there a bank near here?
   ○ Yes. There's one just up the street.
   ★ How far is it?
   ○ About half a block. It's across from the hotel.
3. ★ Excuse me. Is there a gas station near here?
   ○ Yes. There's one just up the street.
   ★ How far is it?
   ○ About two blocks. It's on the corner of Main and West St.
4. ★ Excuse me. Is there a drug store near here?
   ○ Yes. There's one just up the street.
   ★ How far is it?
   ○ About three blocks. It's between the library and the church.
5. ★ Excuse me. Is there a laundromat near here?
   ○ Yes. There's one just up the street.
   ★ How far is it?
   ○ About _____

Practice D
2. ★ What time is the next train to New York?
   ○ At one forty-five. It leaves in half an hour.
   ★ What time does it arrive in New York?
   ○ At four o'clock.
3. ★ What time is the next bus to Los Angeles?
   ○ At eight thirty. It leaves in twenty minutes.
   ★ What time does it arrive in Los Angeles?
   ○ At midnight.
4. ★ What time is the next train to Dallas?
   ○ At nine fifteen. It leaves in ten minutes.
   ★ What time does it arrive in Dallas?
   ○ At noon.

REVIEW: Lessons 1–6, page 13
Which One Is It?
1. b   4. a   7. b
2. a   5. b   8. a
3. a   6. b   9. a

Yes or No?
1. no   3. yes   5. yes   7. no
2. yes   4. no   6. yes   8. yes

Match the Sentences
1. d   3. g   5. c   7. f
2. a   4. b   6. h   8. e

DISCOVER: Lessons 1–6, page 14
Discover A
1. Donna is a dentist.
2. She works in a clinic in Boston.
3. She likes to play tennis.
4. Frank sells clothes.
5. No, she doesn't.
6. She (probably) works during the day.
7. She doesn't like her supervisor.
8. He likes to watch TV.
9. She sleeps during the day because she works at night.
10. Peter is a singer.
11. He works during the night.
12. Yes, he does.

Lesson 7, page 16
Practice B
1. George is a machine operator.
2. He works in a factory on King St.
3. He works eight hours a day.
4. He works forty hours a week.
5. He starts work at eight o'clock.
6. He finishes work at four thirty.
7. He makes ten dollars an hour.

Practice C
2. Where do you work?
3. How many hours do you work a day?
4. What time do you start work?
5. How much money do you make a week?
6. What does Donna do?
7. How many hours does she work a week?
8. What time does she finish work?
9. How much does she make a year?
10. Does she like her job?
11. Are you a teacher?
12. What time do you start school?

Lesson 8, page 18
Practice B
1. She gets up early.
2. She takes the bus and then the subway.
3. It takes her about an hour.
4. She buys a cup of coffee because she is tired.
5. Mr. Davis is angry because she is late.
6. She feels happy after work.
7. She goes for a walk in the park to relax.

Practice C
(i) 2. eat   (ii) 2. study
3. have   3. read
4. start   4. make
5. go   5. buy

Lesson 9, page 20
Practice B
2. ★ How much are those oranges?
   ○ 25¢ each.
   ★ Can you give me six, please?
3. ★ How much is that cake?
   ○ $1.20 a piece.
   ★ Can you give me four pieces, please?
4. ★ How much are those chocolates?
   ○ 50¢ each.
   ★ Can you give me one, please?

Practice C
2. ★ What's your telephone number?
   ○ 936-8459.
   ★ Could you repeat that, please?
   ○ 936-8459.
3. ★ What's your date of birth?
   ○ July 9, 1948.
   ★ Could you repeat that, please?
   ○ July 9, 1948.
4. ★ What's your last name?
   ○ Santos.
   ★ Could you repeat that, please?
   ○ Santos.

Practice D
2. ★ Can you give me that book, please?
   ○ This one?
   ★ No, the black one.
3. ★ Can you give me that apple?
   ○ This one?
   ★ No, the big one.
4. ★ Can you give me that chair, please?
   ○ This one?
   ★ No, the new one.

Practice E
2. speak   4. pass   6. pay
3. sign   5. spell   7. use

Listening Activity
A. 1. She doesn't get up early.
   2. He isn't always late.
   3. What time does he finish work?
   4. How much does she make?
   5. It isn't time to go home.
   6. It takes me an hour to get to work.
B. 1. Yes, he does.
   2. About two blocks north, on Baxter St.
   3. He's a salesman.

Lesson 10, page 22
Practice B
1. It's quiet.
2. It's sunny.
3. There are two bedrooms.
4. It's next to the living room.
5. Six hundred dollars a month.

Practice C
2. How many bedrooms are there?
3. How much is the rent?
4. What floor is the apartment on?
5. What's the neighborhood like?
6. Is there a parking garage?
7. Is there a laundry room?
8. Is there a shower in the bathroom?
9. Is the apartment near the subway?

Lesson 11, page 24
Practice B
2. Put these flowers on the table in the dining room.
3. Put this plant beside the TV in the living room.
4. Put these shoes under the bed in John's bedroom.
5. Put this chair in front of the desk in the office.
6. Put these batteries in the radio over there.
7. Put this book under the telephone on the table.
8. Put these spoons in the tray on the counter.
9. Put this bicycle beside the door in the garage.
10. Put this cream in the refrigerator.
11. Put these gloves on the seat in the car.

Practice C
(i) 2. about   4. at   6. near
3. of   5. at   7. in
(ii) 1. two   3. to
2. to   4. too
(iii) 1. Their   3. There
2. They're   4. there

Lesson 12, page 26
Practice B
2. ★ Can you get me my gloves, please?
   ○ Where are they?
   ★ I think they're in the living room.
   ○ They're not here.
   ★ Look in the bedroom in my bag.
   ○ You're right. They're here.
3. ★ Can you get me my shoes, please?
   ○ Where are they?
   ★ I think they're in the bedroom.
   ○ They're not here.
   ★ Look in the living room under the sofa.
   ○ You're right. They're here.
4. ★ Can you get me the garbage can, please?
   ○ Where is it?
   ★ I think it's in the basement.
   ○ It's not here.
   ★ Look in the garage beside the door.
   ○ You're right. It's here.
5. ★ Can you get my jacket, please?
   ○ Where is it?
   ★ I think it's in the bedroom.
   ○ It's not here.
   ★ Look in the laundry room in the washer.
   ○ You're right. It's here.
6. ★ Can you get me the car keys, please?
   ○ Where are they?
   ★ I think they're in the car.
   ○ They're not here.
   ★ Look in the living room on the TV.
   ○ You're right. They're here.
7. ★ Can you get me the sugar, please?
   ○ Where is it?
   ★ I think it's in the cupboard.
   ○ It's not here.
   ★ Look on the shelf below the cups.
   ○ You're right. It's here.
8. ★ Can you get me the milk, please?
   ○ Where is it?
   ★ I think it's in the refrigerator.
   ○ It's not here.
   ★ Look on the shelf above the cheese.
   ○ You're right. It's here.

Practice C
2. How many children does Maria have?

3. How old is Donna?
4. What does Pat do?
5. What time does the class start?
6. Where is the drugstore?
7. Where are the rooms?
8. How far is the park from here?
9. What time does the bus leave?
10. How much is the rent?
11. How do I get to the airport?

REVIEW: Lessons 7–12, page 27
Where Is It?
1. False   4. False
2. True   5. False
3. False   6. True

Answer the Questions.
1. He gets up at 5:30.
2. He usually has two eggs with toast and black coffee for breakfast.
3. He takes the subway to work.
4. He starts work at 8:00.
5. Yes, he does.
6. He works eight hours.
7. He sometimes eats lunch in a small restaurant near his office.
8. He always eats dinner at his sister's house.
9. He plays cards.
10. He sleeps seven and a half hours.

Make a Sentence.
1. How much do you make an hour?
2. It's time to go to bed.
3. How much is the rent?
4. What's your apartment like?
5. Could you put it on the table?
6. I can't find my new jacket.
7. How do you say this word in English?
8. That's too expensive for me.

DISCOVER: Lessons 7–12, page 28
Discover A
1. b. pots
   c. toaster/blender
2. a. is, stereo
   b. is, in front of
   c. is, armchair
3. a. are, pillows
   b. is, alarm clock
   c. is, beside
4. a. is, bathtub, toilet
   b. is, mirror
   c. are, towels

Lesson 13, page 30
Practice B
1. Because she is tired.
2. Because he is bored.
3. He wants to buy a car.
4. Because he doesn't want to take the subway to work.
5. He wants to be rich.
6. He wants to have a million dollars.
7. He wants to go to Hawaii.

Practice C
2. Where does he want to go?
3. What time do you want to eat dinner?
4. What time does Tom want to leave?
5. What do they want to watch?
6. What does Linda want to drink?

Practice D
2. ★ Why do they want to buy a house?
   ○ Because they don't want to live in an apartment.
3. ★ Why does he want to have a million dollars?
   ○ Because he doesn't want to work.
4. ★ Why does she want to buy a washer?
   ○ Because she doesn't want to go to the laundromat.
5. ★ Why do you want to take a taxi?
   ○ Because I don't want to be late.
6. ★ Why does he want to go to the restaurant?
   ○ Because he doesn't want to cook dinner.

Lesson 14, page 32
Practice B
2. is, She's   5. are, I'm
3. are, They're   6. Are, we're
4. are, They're   7. Is, he's

Practice C
2. ★ Where are you going?
   ○ I'm going to the restaurant. Do you want to come?
   ★ I can't. I'm busy.
   ○ What are you doing?
   ★ I'm studying English.
3. ★ Where are you going?
   ○ I'm going to John's house. Do you want to come?
   ★ I can't. I'm busy.
   ○ What are you doing?
   ★ I'm doing the laundry.
4. ★ Where are you going?
   ○ I'm going to the supermarket. Do you want to come?
   ★ I can't. I'm busy.
   ○ What are you doing?
   ★ I'm cooking dinner.
5. ★ Where are you going?
   ○ I'm going to the library. Do you want to come?
   ★ I can't. I'm busy.
   ○ What are you doing?
   ★ I'm writing a letter.
6. ★ Where are you going?
   ○ I'm going for a walk. Do you want to come?
   ★ I can't. I'm busy.
   ○ What are you doing?
   ★ I'm taking some photos.
7. ★ Where are you going?
   ○ I'm going downtown. Do you want to come?
   ★ I can't. I'm busy.
   ○ What are you doing?
   ★ I'm washing the kitchen floor.

Practice D
2. ★ Where is Mr. Benson?
   ○ He's at school.
   ★ What is he doing?
   ○ He's teaching the English class.
3. ★ Where is Lisa?
   ○ She's at the library.
   ★ What is she doing?
   ○ She's listening to an English cassette.
4. ★ Where are the children?
   ○ They're in the kitchen.
   ★ What are they doing?
   ○ They're eating breakfast.
5. ★ Where are you?
   ○ I'm in the bedroom.
   ★ What are you doing?
   ○ I'm reading a book.
6. ★ Where is your mother?
   ○ She's at the supermarket.
   ★ What is she doing?
   ○ She's buying food for dinner.
7. ★ Where are your parents?
   ○ They're at their friend's house.
   ★ What are they doing?
   ○ They're watching TV.

Lesson 15, page 34
Practice B
2. No, she isn't.   7. No, he isn't.
3. Yes, she is.   8. No, he isn't.
4. No, he isn't.   9. Yes, he is.
5. No, he isn't.   10. No, he isn't.
6. No, he isn't.

Practice D
1. Turn on   5. Turn on
2. Turn off   6. Open
3. Turn off   6. Close
4. Pick up   8. Take out

Listening Activity
A. 1. She's washing the dishes.
   2. He's going to the library.
   3. He wants to be a doctor.
B. 1. yes   4. no
   2. no   5. yes
   3. yes

Lesson 16, page 36
Practice B
1. ★ What are you doing?
   ○ I'm washing the dishes.
   ★ How often do you wash the dishes?
   ○ I wash the dishes once a day.
2. ★ Where are you going?
   ○ I'm going to the library.
   ★ How often do you go to the library?

○ I go to the library once a month.
4. ★ Where are you going?
   ○ I'm going to the dentist.
   ★ How often do you go to the dentist?
   ○ I go to the dentist once every six months.
5. ★ What are you doing?
   ○ I'm cleaning the house.
   ★ How often do you clean the house?
   ○ I clean the house once every two weeks.
6. ★ Where are you going?
   ○ I'm going to my English class.
   ★ How often do you go to your English class?
   ○ I go to my English class twice a week.

Practice C
1. Do
2. Are
3. Is
4. Are
5. Do
6. Is
7. Are
8. Does
9. Does
10. Are

Practice D
2. He's reading, He reads
3. They're eating, eat
4. She's working, works
5. I'm studying, I study
6. Jill is playing, Jill plays

Lesson 17, page 38
Practice B
2. ★ Would you like to go dancing?
   ○ Sure. What time do you want to meet?
   ★ How about nine fifteen?
   ○ That's fine. Where do you want to meet?
   ★ Can we meet at your house?
   ○ OK. See you later!
3. ★ Would you like to go to the park?
   ○ Sure. What time do you want to meet?
   ★ How about two thirty?
   ○ That's fine. Where do you want to meet?
   ★ Can we meet on the corner of King and West Street?
   ○ OK. See you later!
4. ★ Would you like to go to a restaurant?
   ○ Sure. What time do you want to meet?
   ★ How about seven thirty?
   ○ That's fine. Where do you want to meet?
   ★ Can we meet at the Seaside restaurant?
   ○ OK. See you later!
5. ★ Would you like to go shopping?
   ○ Sure. What time do you want to meet?
   ★ How about one o'clock?
   ○ That's fine. Where do you want to meet?
   ★ Can we meet in front of the supermarket?
   ○ OK. See you later!

Practice C
2. ★ Would you like an apple?
   ○ No, thanks, but I'd like an orange.
3. ★ Would you like some bread?
   ○ No, thanks, but I'd like some cake.
4. ★ Would you like some salad?
   ○ No, thanks, but I'd like some soup.
5. ★ Would you like a banana?
   ○ No, thanks, but I'd like a glass of water.

Practice D
2. ★ Would you like something to drink?
   ○ I'd like some orange juice, please.
3. ★ Would you like something to eat?
   ○ I'd like some cheese, please.

4. ★ Would you like something to drink?
   ○ I'd like a cup of coffee, please.
5. ★ Would you like something to eat?
   ○ I'd like a chicken sandwich, please.

Lesson 18, page 40
Practice B
2. ★ Can you give me my pen, please?
   ○ Which one is yours?
   ★ The black one behind the telephone.
3. ★ Can you give me my dictionary, please?
   ○ Which one is yours?
   ★ The small one on the chair.
4. ★ Can you give me my pencil, please?
   ○ Which one is yours?
   ★ The blue one under the book.

Practice C
2. ★ I'm looking for Susan Bennett.
   ○ She over there. She's wearing the dark sunglasses.
3. ★ I'm looking for the supervisor.
   ○ He's over there. He's wearing the black jacket.
4. ★ I'm looking for Mr. Lee.
   ○ He's over there. He's wearing the blue sweater.

Practice D
2. Which apple do you want?
3. Which pen is yours?
4. Whose pen is this?
5. Who is that over there?
6. Who is that woman wearing the blue dress?

Practice E
1. my   4. mine   7. her
2. hers   5. yours   8. his
3. his   6. my

REVIEW Lessons 13–18, page 41
Which One Is It?
1. a   4. b   7. a
2. a   5. b   8. b
3. b   6. a   9. a

What's the Answer?
1. a   5. a   9. b
2. a   6. b   10. a
3. b   7. a   11. a
4. a   8. a   12. b

DISCOVER: Lessons 13–18, page 42
Discover A
1. beige cotton, red nylon, brown suede
2. dark blue wool, light blue silk, purple

Discover D
1. ★ I like it a lot. What material is it?
   ○ It's wool.
   ★ I like the color, too.
   ○ Thanks. I have a skirt the same color at home.
2. ★ What are you wearing to the party tonight?
   ○ I don't know. Maybe my new suit. What about you?
   ★ Nothing special. Just blue jeans and a shirt.
3. ★ Who's the woman over there?
   ○ Which one?
   ★ The one wearing the dark green dress.
   ○ Oh, that's my sister.
   ★ She's very attractive.
   ○ Yes, and she's married, too.

Lesson 19, page 44
Practice B
2. Give it to them.
3. Give them to him.
4. Give it to us.
5. Give it to her.
6. Give it to him.
7. Give them to us.
8. Give them to her.

Practice C
2. ★ Give this money to the cashier in room one.
   ○ Where's room one?
   ★ Go down the hall. It's the first room on the left.

3. ★ Give this book to the teacher in room fifteen.
   ○ Where's room fifteen?
   ★ Go down the hall. It's the third room on the left.

Practice D
2. ★ Give this jacket to the man in the white shirt.
   ○ What's his name?
   ★ Mr. Davis.
3. ★ Give this suitcase to the woman in the green sweater.
   ○ What's her name?
   ★ Ms. Wilson.

Lesson 20, page 46
Practice B
2. ★ What's your occupation?
   ○ I'm a cashier.
   ★ How many years experience do you have?
   ○ Two years.
   ★ We'll pay you $4 an hour. Are you interested?
   ○ Yes, I am.
   ★ Can you start tonight?
   ○ Yes, I can.
3. ★ What's your occupation?
   ○ I'm a secretary.
   ★ How many years experience do you have?
   ○ Four years.
   ★ We'll pay you $250 a week. Are you interested?
   ○ Yes, I am.
   ★ Can you start tomorrow?
   ○ Yes, I can.
4. ★ What's your occupation?
   ○ I'm a truck driver.
   ★ How many years experience do you have?
   ○ Fifteen years.
   ★ We'll pay you $10.50 an hour. Are you interested?
   ○ Yes, I am.
   ★ Can you start next Tuesday?
   ○ Yes, I can.

Practice C
2. Do you have a car?
3. Can you work on Saturdays?
4. Are you a mechanic?
5. Are you a student?
6. Do you need a mechanic to repair your trucks?
7. Do you have an appointment at 3:00?
8. Can you start next Monday?
9. Are you interested in this job?
10. Can you speak Spanish?

Lesson 21, page 48
Practice B
2. ★ When will the children be home?
   ○ They'll be home later.
3. ★ When will Mr. Davis be home?
   ○ He'll be home tonight.
4. ★ When will you be home?
   ○ I'll be home in two hours.
5. ★ When will you and Tom be home?
   ○ We'll be home next week.
6. ★ When will your mother be home?
   ○ She'll be home in about ten minutes.

Practice C
1. ★ Will Mr. Davis be in tomorrow?
   ○ No, he won't be in until next Friday.
3. ★ Will you be in early this evening?
   ○ No, I won't be in until late tonight.
4. ★ Will the students be in this afternoon?
   ○ No, they won' be in until tomorrow morning.
5. ★ Will the dentist be in next week?
   ○ No, he won't be in until next month.
6. ★ Will you and your husband be in at six o'clock?
   ○ No, we won't be in until eight.

Listening Activity
A. 1. We'll be there in an hour.
   2. They'll try again later.
   3. They won't arrive until tomorrow.

4. They want to arrive tomorrow.
5. She can't start next Thursday.
6. He can come here on Saturday.
B. 1. 518 626-5729
   2. his mother
   3. yes
   4. his mother
   5. the operator

Lesson 22, page 50
Practice B
3. I'll get it.   7. I'll ask them.
4. I'll help her.   8. I'll get them.
5. I'll help you.   9. I'll call you.
6. I'll tell him.   10. I'll ask him.

Practice C
2. ★ I can't come to work tomorrow.
   ○ Why not?
   ★ Because I have to go to the dentist.
3. ★ I can't go to a movie tonight.
   ○ Why not?
   ★ Because I have to do the laundry.
4. ★ I can't go dancing with you.
   ○ Why not?
   ★ Because I have to meet my boyfriend.
5. ★ I can't go shopping.
   ○ Why not?
   ★ Because I have to study English.
6. ★ I can't help you now.
   ○ Why not?
   ★ Because I have to make dinner.
7. ★ I can't finish this now.
   ○ Why not?
   ★ Because I have to go home.

Practice D
2. ★ Will you be at school the day after tomorrow?
   ○ No, I won't be there.
3. ★ Will you be at the dance tonight?
   ○ Yes, I'll be there.
4. ★ Will you be at the library this afternoon?
   ○ Yes, I'll be there.
5. ★ Will you be home soon?
   ○ No, I won't be there.
6. ★ Will you be at the restaurant later?
   ○ Yes, I'll be there.

Lesson 23, page 52
Practice B
2. ★ Can you give this to Mr. Smith?
   ○ I can't right now. I'm too busy.
   ★ When can you do it?
   ○ I can do it this afternoon.
3. ★ Can you take this to room ten?
   ○ I can't right now. I'm too busy.
   ★ When can you do it?
   ○ I can do it in half an hour.
4. ★ Can you make dinner?
   ○ I can't right now. I'm too busy.
   ★ When can you do it?
   ○ I can do it later.
5. ★ Can you wash the dishes?
   ○ I can't. I'm too busy.
   ★ When can you do it?
   ○ I can do it in a couple of minutes.

Practice C
2. ★ Can Jeff and Nora go to the party?
   ○ No, they can't. They have to work.
3. ★ Can Susan go for a walk with us?
   ○ No, she can't. She has to do the laundry.
4. ★ Can you and Bill go to a movie tonight?
   ○ No, we can't. We have to clean our apartment.
5. ★ Can Mr. Benson have dinner with us tonight?
   ○ No, he can't. He has to meet somebody.
6. ★ Can the secretary type this letter?
   ○ No, she / he can't. She / He has to go home.

Practice D
2. Where does he have to go?
3. What time do they have to be there?
4. Why do you have to stay home?
5. What time does your wife have to be at work?
6. Who does he have to call?
7. Where do you have to go?
8. Why does she have to sell her car?

Lesson 24, page 54
Practice B
2. shouldn't worry
3. should drink
4. should put
5. shouldn't eat
6. shouldn't go
7. should take
8. should go
9. should get
10. should buy

Practice C
2. ★ How long have you been in New York?
   ○ Three months.
3. ★ How long have you been a mechanic?
   ○ Ten years.
4. ★ How long have you been sick?
   ○ Five days.
5. ★ How long have you been in this English class?
   ○ _____

Practice D
2. speak
3. to fill out
4. take
5. to get off
6. make
7. to stay
8. to visit
9. meet

REVIEW: Lessons 19–24, page 55
Which One Is It?
1. b   4. b   7. a
2. a   5. b   8. b
3. b   6. a   9. b

Yes or No?
1. yes   5. no   8. yes
2. no   6. yes   9. no
3. yes   7. no   10. yes
4. yes

Finish the Conversations.
1. Is, is   5. Will, won't
2. Does, doesn't 6. Does, doesn't
3. Are, Aren't   7. Can, can't
4. Can, can't   8. Is, isn't

DISCOVER: Lessons 19–24, page 56
Discover A
2. ★ You shouldn't eat rich food.
3. ★ What's the matter?
   ○ I have a cold.
   ★ You should take vitamin C and drink lots of liquids.
4. ★ What's the matter?
   ○ I have a toothache.
   ★ You should call the dentist.
5. ★ What's the matter?
   ○ I have a sore back.
   ★ You should bend your knees when you lift heavy things.
6. ★ What's the matter?
   ○ I have sore feet.
   ★ You should rest and wear comfortable shoes.

Discover B
○ I know, doctor. I can't sleep.
★ Why can't you sleep?
○ Because I have a headache and my stomach is upset.
★ How long have you been sick like this?
○ For about a week.
★ Are you taking any medicine?
○ No, I'm not.
★ Take this prescription to the drugstore. They will give you some medicine for your problem.

Lesson 25, page 58
Practice B (Answers will vary.)
2. ★ What's the weather like today?
   ○ Terrible. It's cold and snowing.
3. ★ What's the weather like today?
   ○ So-so. It's raining but it's warm.
4. ★ What's the weather like today?
   ○ Terrible. It's hot and cloudy.
5. ★ What's the weather like today?
   ○ Terrible. It's cold and windy.

6. ★ What's the weather like today?
   ○ So-so. It's cool and foggy.
Practice C
2. was   5. is   8. will be
3. will be   6. was   9. is
4. will be   7. was   10. was

Lesson 26, page 60
Practice A (ii)
2. ★ Is the bus to Chicago on time?
   ○ No, I'm sorry. That bus is delayed.
   ★ What time will it leave?
   ○ At nine thirty.
3. ★ Is the train to Washington on time?
   ○ No, I'm sorry. That train is delayed.
   ★ What time will it leave?
   ○ At eleven forty-five.

Practice B (ii)
2. ★ Do you have a double room with an air conditioner?
   ○ Yes, we do. Would you like a room with a balcony?
   ★ It doesn't matter, but I'd like a room at the back.
3. ★ Do you have a single room with a shower?
   ○ Yes, we do. Would you like a room at the front?
   ★ It doesn't matter, but I'd like a room with a color TV.

Practice C (ii)
2. ★ Could you send a taxi to 3507 Lake Road, please?
   ○ Is that an apartment?
   ★ Yes, it's apartment number 52. How long will it take?
   ○ About half an hour.
3. ★ Could you send a taxi to 553 Sunset Avenue?
   ○ Is that an apartment?
   ★ No, it's a house. How long will it take?
   ○ About 15 minutes.

Lesson 27, page 62
Practice B
2. ★ When is your vacation?
   ○ In two weeks.
   ★ Are you going to Japan?
   ○ No, I'm going to Hong Kong. I went to Japan two years ago.
3. ★ When is your vacation?
   ○ Next August.
   ★ Are you going to France?
   ○ No, I'm going to Germany. I went to France last year.

Practice C
2. ★ Did you go to France two years ago?
   ○ No, I didn't.
   ★ Where did you go?
   ○ I went to Germany.
3. ★ Did you go to a movie last night?
   ○ No, I didn't.
   ★ Where did you go?
   ○ I went to a party.

Practice D
2. had
3. met
4. are
5. were
6. meet
7. buy
8. went

Practice E
2. ★ Where did you go yesterday?
   ○ I went to the camera store.
   ★ What did you buy?
   ○ I bought some color film.
   ★ How much did you pay?
   ○ I paid five dollars.
3. ★ Where did you go yesterday?
   ○ I went to the furniture store.
   ★ What did you buy?
   ○ I bought a sofa.
   ★ How much did you pay?
   ○ I paid four hundred fifty dollars.
4. ★ Where did you go yesterday?
   ○ I went to the clothing store.
   ★ What did you buy?
   ○ I bought a jacket.
   ★ How much did you pay?
   ○ I paid seventy-nine dollars.

Listening Activity
A. 1. we're   6. want
   2. were   7. won't
   3. where   8. work
   4. when   9. walk
   5. went   10. wear
B. 1. They went to New York City.
   2. They went to Central Park.
   3. It was beautiful.
   4. They met Nancy's uncle.
   5. No, they didn't.
   6. They had lunch at a sidewalk cafe.
   7. They paid $20 each for lunch.
   8. Linda bought a book about New York City.
   9. It was $10.

Lesson 28, page 64
Practice B
1. They stayed in Mexico for two weeks.
2. They started their trip on the Pacific coast.
3. They started there because they wanted to relax in the sun.
4. They stayed in a small hotel.
5. They sat by the pool and talked, ate tropical fruits and drank different fruit juices.
6. They went to the desert.
7. They drove.
8. They walked around the town and looked at the old buildings.
9. They bought souvenirs in the market.
10. They saw many interesting animals and trees.
11. They felt tired, but happy.
12. Yes, they had a good time.

Practice C
2. ★ Did you start on the Atlantic coast?
   ○ No, I started on the Pacific coast.
3. ★ Did you stay in a big hotel?
   ○ No, I stayed in a small hotel.
4. ★ Did you eat American food?
   ○ No, I ate Mexican food.
5. ★ Did you rent a motorcycle?
   ○ No, I rented a car.
6. ★ Did you drive to Mexico City?
   ○ No, I drove to a town in the mountains.
7. ★ Did you buy souvenirs in your hotel?
   ○ No, I bought souvenirs in the market.
8. ★ Did you take photos of the people?
   ○ No, I took photos of the buildings.
9. ★ Did you see many tourists?
   ○ No, I saw only Mexicans.
10. ★ Did you feel unhappy about your trip?
   ○ No, we felt happy.

Lesson 29, page 66
Practice B
2. ★ Where were you last week?
   ○ I was in Miami.
   ★ How long were you there?
   ○ For a week.
   ★ Was your mother with you?
   ○ No, she wasn't. She was in Dallas.
3. ★ Where were you last night?
   ○ I was at a party.
   ★ How long were you there?
   ○ For two hours.
   ★ Was your husband with you?
   ○ No, he wasn't. He was at home.
4. ★ Where were you yesterday?
   ○ I was at the beach.
   ★ How long were you there?
   ○ For a few hours.
   ★ Were your children with you?
   ○ No, they were at school.

Practice D
2. ★ What did you give to your husband?
   ○ I gave him a new shirt.
3. ★ What did you send to your grandparents?
   ○ I sent them a postcard.
4. ★ What did you get for your daughter?
   ○ I got her a bicycle.

5. ★ What did you send to Mr. Badali?
   ○ I sent him an application form.
6. ★ What did you buy for your aunt?
   ○ I bought her a new blouse.
7. ★ What did you give to the children?
   ○ I gave them some money.

Lesson 30, page 68
Practice B
1. Mary is going to visit her sister in California.
2. Nora and Jeff are going to Haiti.
3. Jeff is going to take photos of the people and old architecture.
4. They are going to visit a friend.
5. Their friend works in a health clinic.
6. They are going to rent a jeep.
7. Because the clinic is in the mountains and the roads are in bad condition.

Practice D
2. When is Maria going to make dinner?
3. When are you going to visit me?
4. When is Tom going to fix his car?
5. When are they going to sell their house?
6. When are we going to go dancing?

Practice E
3. We drove
4. They saw
5. She is going to take
6. she took
7. We are going to see
8. He is going to rent
9. I left
10. They ate

REVIEW: Lessons 25–30, page 69
Which One Is It?
1. a   4. b   7. b
2. b   5. b   8. b
3. b   6. a   9. a

Yes or No?
1. no   4. yes   7. no
2. yes   5. no   8. no
3. no   6. no   9. yes

Finish the Conversations.
1. Do, don't
2. Did, didn't
3. Did, didn't
4. Does, doesn't
5. Is, isn't
6. Are, aren't
7. Did, didn't
8. Does, doesn't
9. Is, isn't
10. Do, don't

DISCOVER: Lessons 25–30, page 70
Discover A
2. ★ Did you wear....
   ○ No, I didn't. I wore a dress.
3. ★ Did you make....
   ○ No, I didn't. I made fish for dinner.
4. ★ Did you speak....
   ○ No, I didn't. I spoke English to the teacher.
5. ★ Did you come....
   ○ No, I didn't. I came to New York by train.
6. ★ Did you do....
   ○ No, I didn't. I did my laundry last night.
7. ★ Did you forget....
   ○ No, I didn't. I forgot my umbrella.
8. ★ Did you write....
   ○ No, I didn't. I wrote to Mary.
9. ★ Did you live....
   ○ No, I didn't. I lived in a house.
10. ★ Did you study....
   ○ No, I didn't. I studied psychology at the university.
11. ★ Did you finish....
   ○ No, I didn't. I finished work at 6:30.
12. ★ Did you wait....
   ○ No, I didn't. I waited in front of the restaurant.

Discover B
1. lived
2. do, stayed, studied
3. wait, waited
4. were, forgot, had to

Lesson 31, page 72
Practice B
2. ★ I'm going to type this letter.
   ○ Sit down, I'll type it for you.
   ★ Oh, thank you.
3. ★ I'm going to wash the dishes.
   ○ Sit down. I'll wash them for you.
   ★ Oh, thank you.
4. ★ I'm going to get the newspaper.
   ○ Sit down. I'll get it for you.
   ★ Oh, thank y ou.
5. ★ I'm going to call the children.
   ○ Sit down. I'll call them for you.
   ★ Oh, thank you.
6. ★ I'm going to make dinner.
   ○ Sit down. I'll make it for you.
   ★ Oh, thank you.

Practice C
2. ★ My refrigerator isn't working.
   ○ OK. I'll check it for you.
   ★ How much will it cost?
   ○ Fifty-five dollars.
   ★ I can't afford that.
   ○ Sorry, I can't do it for less.
   ★ OK. I'll think about it and let you know tomorrow.
3. ★ My brakes aren't working.
   ○ OK. I'll check them for you.
   ★ How much will it cost?
   ○ Two hundred and thirty dollars.
   ★ I can't afford that.
   ○ Sorry, I can't do it for less.
   ★ OK. I'll think about it and let you know tomorrow.
4. ★ My watch isn't working.
   ○ OK. I'll check it for you.
   ★ How much will it cost?
   ○ Forty dollars.
   ★ I can't afford that.
   ○ Sorry I can't do it for less.
   ★ OK. I'll think about it and let you know tomorrow.

Practice D
1. have, come, bring
2. do, fix, need, bring
3. visit, know, need, take

Lesson 32, page 74
Practice B
1. He saw a sports jacket.
2. They were at the front of the store.
3. It cost $85.
4. He looked at the label to check the size and the material.
5. The jacket was 100% wool.
6. The jacket looked great.
7. Yes, John bought it.
8. He paid for the jacket by cash.

Practice C
2. ★ I'm going to order some soup. What about you?

○ I think I'll have a hamburger.
3. ★ I'm going to watch TV. What about you?
   ○ I think I'll study English.
4. ★ I'm going to clean the house. What about you?
   ○ I think I'll go to bed.

Practice D
2. Try it on.
3. Try them on.
4. Turn it on.
5. Take them off.
6. Put it on.
7. Pick them up.

Lesson 33, page 76
Practice B
2. Where are the children's clothes?
3. What size do you wear?
4. How does it look?
5. Where did you buy your dress?
6. Is this store open on Saturdays?
7. Are you going to buy it?
8. Did you go shopping on the weekend?
9. Is it 100% cotton?
10. Do you have this dress in a different color?

Practice C
2. ★ How do those pants fit?
   ○ They're too long. Do you have a smaller size?
   ★ Yes, I'll get them for you.
3. ★ How does that hat fit?
   ○ It's too small. Do you have a bigger size?
   ★ Yes, I'll get it for you.
4. ★ How do those gloves fit?
   ○ They're too big. Do you have a smaller size?
   ★ Yes, I'll get it for you.
5. ★ How does that skirt fit?
   ○ It's too loose. Do you have a smaller size?
   ★ Yes, I'll get it for you.
6. ★ How does that belt fit?
   ○ It's too tight. Do you have a bigger size?
   ★ Yes, I'll get it for you.

Listening Activity
A. 1. I'm going to have a sandwich.
   2. I'll think about it.
   3. I'd like to try them on.
   4. I can't afford that.
   5. I'll turn it on for you.
   6. I think I'll take off my jacket.
B. 1. The red dress is cheaper.
   2. It's $37.
   3. It's $2,500.
   4. No, he can't.
   5. They're size 5½.
   6. Yes, she does.
   7. The lights don't work.
   8. No, he can't.

Lesson 34, page 78
Practice A (ii)
2. ★ Can you lend me a dollar?
   ○ What for?
   ★ I want to buy a bus ticket.
   ○ When can you pay me back?

★ Tomorrow morning.
○ OK.
3. ★ Can you lend me twenty dollars?
   ○ What for?
   ★ I want to buy a shirt.
   ○ When can you pay me back?
   ★ Next Thursday.
   ○ OK.
4. ★ Can you lend me a thousand dollars?
   ○ What for?
   ★ I want to buy a car.
   ○ When can you pay me back?
   ★ In six months.
   ○ OK.

Practice B (ii)
2. ★ How much is this sofa?
   ○ It's four hundred dollars, and that one is six hundred dollars.
   ★ Why is this one less expensive?
   ○ Because it's on sale.
3. ★ How much is this carpet?
   ○ It's two thousand dollars, and that one is eighteen hundred dollars.
   ★ Why is this one less expensive?
   ○ Because it's on sale.
4. ★ How much is this cassette player?
   ○ It's one hundred twenty dollars, and that one is ninety-five dollars.
   ★ Why is this one less expensive?
   ○ Because it's on sale.

Practice C (ii)
2. ★ I'd like to return this blouse.
   ○ What's wrong with it?
   ★ Two buttons are missing.
   ○ Would you like an exchange or a refund?
   ★ An exchange, please.
3. ★ I'd like to return this dress.
   ○ What's wrong with it?
   ★ My wife doesn't like the color.
   ○ Would you like an exchange or a refund?
   ★ An exchange, please.

Lesson 35, page 80
Practice B
2. ★ Where is the flour?
   ○ It's in the baking needs section, aisle two on the right.
3. ★ Where are the carrots?
   ○ They're in the vegetable section, aisle one on the left.
4. ★ Where is the cheese?
   ○ It's in the dairy section, aisle one on the right.
5. ★ Where is the steak?
   ○ It's in the meat section, aisle three on the left.
6. ★ Where are the frozen dinners?
   ○ They're in the frozen food section, aisle three on the right.
7. ★ Where is the apple juice?

○ It's in the beverage section, aisle one on the right.

Practice C
2. How much tea do you drink?
3. How many apples do you have?
4. How much sugar do you want?
5. How much money do you make?
6. How many eggs do you use?
7. How many stamps do you need?
8. How much time do you have?

Practice D
2. I drink a lot of milk, but I don't drink much coffee.
3. I buy a lot of carrots, but I don't buy many tomatoes.
4. I eat a lot of fish, but I don't eat much meat.
5. I read a lot of books, but I don't read many magazines.

Lesson 36, page 82
Practice B
2. I don't need any money.
3. I don't want anything to drink.
4. I don't have any photos of my family.
6. I didn't send any flowers to my mother.
7. I didn't buy anything for my wife.
8. I didn't have any problems.

Practice C
1. any
2. some
3. anything
4. any, some
5. some
6. anything
7. any
8. some, any
9. something, any
10. anything, a
11. an

REVIEW: Lessons 31–36, page 83
Which One Is It?
1. a
2. a
3. b
4. b
5. a
6. b
7. b
8. b
9. a

What Number Is It?
4
3
2
1

Finish These Conversations.
1. much, in, can't, sorry, it about
2. me, to, back, don't, won't

DISCOVER: Lessons 31–36, page 84
Discover A
1. engine, fix, it
2. flat, one
3. have, oil leak, afford
4. headlight, need

Discover B
2. jar
3. can
4. bar
5. box
6. loaf
7. can / bottle
8. bag / box